Deborah Copaken Kogan

ABOUT THE AUTHOR

ANNE ROIPHE is the author of seventeen books, including *Fruitful*, which was a finalist for the 1996 National Book Award. She has written for the *New York Times*, the *New York Observer*, *Vogue*, *Elle*, *Redbook*, *Parents*, and *The Guardian*, and is a contributing editor to the *Jerusalem Report*. She lives in New York City.

EPILOGUE

A MEMOIR

Anne Roiphe

HARPER PERENNIAL

NEW YORK • LONDON • TORONTO • SYDNEY • NEW DELHI • AUCKLAND

HARPER PERENNIAL

A hardcover edition of this book was published in 2008 by
HarperCollins Publishers.

HarperCollins books may be purchased for educational, business, or
sales promotional use. For information please write: Special Markets
Department, HarperCollins Publishers, 10 East 53rd Street, New
York, NY 10022.

FIRST HARPER PERENNIAL EDITION PUBLISHED 2009.

Designed by Leah Carlson-Stanisic and Emily Taff

Library of Congress Cataloging-in-Publication Data is available
upon request.

ISBN 978-0-06-125463-5

09 10 11 12 13   ID/RRD   10 9 8 7 6 5 4 3 2 1

To:
Daniel
Zachary
Rachel
Violet
Ella
WHO CONTINUE

EACH MONTH THE MOON WAXES AND WANES, GROWS FULL and curves into itself and becomes again a sliver of light against the dark sky. Each month the moon moves across the night, larger and smaller, crescent and full, three quarters of the way, traveling back to the beginning. The tides come in with the gravitational pull of the moon and then they recede as it sends its rays down onto the swelling waters even when human eyes are closed. So time is marked. The tide pirates the dunes away from the shore. The sand returns elsewhere, another village, another beach perhaps thousands of miles away on the shore of another continent.

Time is the widow's friend, they say. But what they say is not always true. What I know is that time is moving forward while the face of the moon changes and changes back again and I am here suspended in time, like the fly I saw in an amber stone, waiting for release.

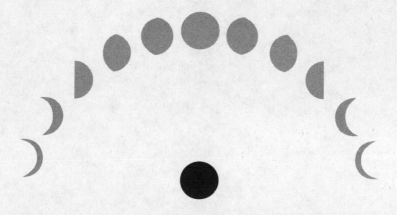

This is a book about happiness regained—or not.

TEN O'CLOCK AT NIGHT, THERE I AM STANDING AT THE front door of my apartment. I have a key but will not use it. Instead I turn the knob, because I have left the door unlocked. I left it unlocked because I wasn't sure I could make the key work. For the thirty-nine years of our marriage my husband always pulled out his key and opened the door when we returned from an evening out. During the day I left the door unlocked. We had a doorman. I trusted my neighbors. I found keys (so subject to loss, so hard sometimes to turn, was it right or left that it should go?) a man's responsibility. Was this a sexual reading of the act, a pun of the unconscious? Perhaps. But now, more significantly, it was a protest against the loss of something far more necessary than a key: my husband, H.

. . .

It was not a beautiful bonzai. It was a scraggly dwarf of a few twigs that still held their green needles. Two of the branches were bare. Nearby there was a small stone and a tiny gray statue of a Chinese man, fishing. He wore a wide-brimmed peasant hat. My youngest daughter had given this plant to H. for Father's Day two years ago. He had nursed it with Miracle-Gro, watered it daily. He shifted it around to catch the sunlight. He carried it with us to our beach home. He put fresh dirt at the four-inch porcelain Chinese man's feet every few months. This bonzai had not died. It hadn't thrived either. I wanted to throw it out. He protested. Don't kill a living plant. Now brown needles fall from some of the branches. Today I throw it out. I know it's still alive. It carries with it his affection. But no matter what I do, each day more needles fall. I do not have the gift. I do not love this stunted plant.

Grief is in two parts. The first is loss. The second is the remaking of life. This book is about the second. Although the division between the two parts is not a line, a wall or a chasm. Think of grief as a river that finally runs into the ocean where it is absorbed but not dissolved, pebbles, moss, fish, twigs from the smallest upland stream run with it and finally float in the salt sea from which life emerged.

I am now a single woman. There is no one at home to call when I am away. Self-pity is never useful. It tends to distort like a fun-house mirror. Nevertheless I indulge myself—heavy helpings of self-pity. Then I stop.

I am going out on a date. I have spoken to a stranger, a man, and arranged to meet him for lunch at a café a few blocks from my building. He sent me a letter in response to a personal advertisement my grown daughters placed for me in the *New York Review of Books*. It said that I was a writer. It said that I was attractive. They think so or else they were lying. They said that I loved the ocean and books. That was true. I didn't read the ad. I was embarrassed. But I was pleased they placed it. Why not? Who knows what waits for me out there among the throngs of divorced and wifeless hordes who might be willing to meet me over the hill? Once I had read in an Edmund Wilson essay of his dislike of women past menopause. He said they were like dried fruits, withered on the vine. The juice was gone. I understood what he meant. Although the words stabbed my heart even then, before I was forty. *What about your juice?* I had written in the margins of the book. But I knew that crones were female and old men were kings, stallions, and producers of heirs. Saul Bellow had a baby at the age of eighty-three. He didn't live long enough after that for her to play Cordelia to his Lear.

The stranger had written a charming letter. He loved books. He loved music. He had wanted to be a writer but had become a public relations executive. He was divorced and he was sixty-nine years old. His letter was on gray stationery with a red border. I will call him P.J. I phoned. His voice was very hoarse and faint. He told me he had reached up to a shelf in his closet for a suitcase that was filled with old books and it had fallen on his throat. I thought about beloved books stored in a suitcase. I agreed to a Sunday lunch.

The stranger met me at a bistro around my corner. I saw him approach. He was short and thin and he had a white mustache. He had a gait that was something like a trot. Like a pony, he moved steadily toward me. We ate our salads and talked. His hands were very veined and age-spotted. I didn't mind, but he didn't seem to be sixty-nine and a lie is like a broken step on the stairway to heaven. His voice was so weak that I had to lean into his space in order to hear his words. He told me he loved Proust and Stendhal and Thomas Mann. He had been divorced ten years. He didn't want to tell me why. His hands shook and trembled. Did he have a disease or was he nervous? He never had any children. He wanted to retire to the Caribbean. He told me that customs had changed since I was a girl and asked me if I understood what was expected in today's dating world. His hand was on my knee. His other hand was stroking my arm up and down as if it were a horse's nose. We had known each other for exactly twenty-five minutes. How does a suitcase on a closet shelf fall on a throat? I tried to imagine it.

The stranger told me about his love of Melville. I am prone to like men who like Melville. He told me he had grown up poor in New Jersey and won a scholarship to Oberlin College. I like men who made themselves, men from families that spoke another language, that had worked hard so their children could have a better life. I moved my chair a little away from him to discourage all the stroking. He moved his chair after me. We talked about Billy Budd for a while. He asked me what I was working on. I told him. He seemed interested. He ordered dessert. I ordered another iced tea. His leg was shaking. I could feel it under the table, a steady tapping on the floor.

As I sipped my iced tea with P.J. and talked about the soldiers in Iraq and discovered that his politics and mine were identical, I realized that the man sitting opposite me was not my husband but a strange man whose hand was approaching my left breast. I pulled my chair back again. He pulled his closer.

I had looked at myself in the full-length mirror. I took in the scar on my left breast from the three operations for benign cysts that appeared over the years—each time with alarm, false alarm and days of renewed promise in the goodness of life. I saw that my body was soft and the skin from my upper arms hung in small ripples. I saw that my legs, once my pride and joy, had blue veins, at least on the back of my right calf. Like Father William, I was old and sagged where once I had been taut and firm. I noticed the folds under my chin. I noticed that my eyebrows had faded away. I saw that a face-lift might help. But I would never do that. It's one thing to wash your face and quite another to cut it, or allow someone else to cut it. Each wrinkle, each line, each tilt of the eye belonged to me, contained the life I had led, the sadness of loss, the pleasure of birth, the wonder of the landscape, the pleasure of flying in the clouds in a four-seater plane at sunset, the cold of the lake in Maine where I learned to dive. Many of my friends had (what they called) work done, pouches under the eyes removed, excess fat pulled off and tucked behind the ears. They did look younger than I but they also did not look quite like themselves. Their expressions seemed pulled across their face as if they were on strings.

I knew that my beatnik style of no-style had long ago gone out of style. I had mostly given that up when I married H. I wore heels as high as my back would allow, believed in artifice, but only of the kind that caused no pain and would wash off in the shower. If I was old now, then so be it. Nature made it so and biology is not a personal enemy, just a fact. I would not insult it, or defy it. I was a perfectly normal old woman and so it would stay.

After all, the men I might meet on my way would have many folds, little hair, muscles that didn't ripple, legs that could go just so far, and eyes that might need cataract operations, as well as prostates that interfered with their sitting through a movie. They too might have had a skin cancer removed, leaving a barely visible dent on their nose just like mine. True enough most of them will feel entitled to a younger beauty, a woman who can glow in the dark. But that changes nothing. I am a rock worn by years of incoming and outgoing tides. There are snails and crabs and tiny bait fish, dark green moss, seaweed bubbles, pebbles, a few shells, perhaps a mermaid scale, or an abandoned beer bottle in my crevices. I have been salted, pickled, brined, so be it.

The stranger called for the check. He insisted on paying. I am used to a man doing that. That's why I never order an expensive dish. My father told me it is a dead giveaway that a woman is a gold digger if she orders lobster or steak. The espresso cups rattled in their saucers as the man stood up; the uneaten biscotti the color of rock and sand sat on a plate. I stood up. Suddenly the man has his spider arms around me and there in the café, with people at every table, he grabs me to him, holds me close and rubs his hands up and down my spine, kisses my mouth so I can hardly breathe, and slips his hands down the front of my blouse. Then he stops. "Was that good for you?" he says. "It was good for me," he adds. I laugh. This was not a nervous laugh. "Are you laughing at me?" he said. "I am," I said, and that was that.

. . .

Our daughters K. and B. have children of their own. One is a writer, one is a law professor. One is married, the other is getting divorced. These sisters are close. This means that a jungle of history lies between them, tying them together, binding them up. My stepdaughter J. is a psychoanalyst, a doctor, like her father, older than the others. But present in their lives, in my life: a necessity. Then there is E. She is the daughter from my first marriage, adopted by H. at the age of five. E. is a falling star, falling into drugs, falling into trouble, falling into AIDS, a brain wired for despair, but shining all the way, sparkling even, love glowing, on occasion dazzling. She writes too. This description applies as well to her biological father, perhaps not the loving part. When H. first met my daughter he knew she was a little girl with mile-wide rips in the soul. After a few months of our being with each other H. told me he hoped he could save her, that together we could save her. We didn't, but we tried mightily.

K. and B. took a taxi together from Brooklyn, where they live a half a block apart from each other, the night my husband died. They appeared in the emergency room and wept. One took my husband's Timex watch off his wrist and put it on her own. One stayed with me in my bed when we finally returned to the apartment in the early hours of the morning. J. spoke to the interns and doctors. She was the color of slate. Dark shadows appeared under her eyes but she seemed to know what to do. She (or was it her husband?) arranged for the funeral home to come to the hospital and retrieve the body. I was able to understand everything but unable to speak.

E. does not come to the funeral. She lives in Minne-
apolis. She has no photo identification, so she cannot get
on the airplane. She has lost the copy of her birth certifi-
cate I had sent. She has misplaced her passport. She has no
driver's license. She wants to come but can't. I know she is
grieving in her own grieving way. I know how she and H.
were together. I know how he cried when he thought she
might die: breath pulled in, choked off, sounds, deep in his
throat.

·   ·   ·

After great sorrow a formal feeling comes, so said Emily
Dickinson. I think she must have been talking about the
quiet and stillness that fills the mind, protecting it from inner storms, from bouts of fear. Not thinking is like pulling
the blanket up over one's head to avoid seeing the monsters
in the room. It is like being on a train and watching the
landscape sweep by, farm, granary, woods, path, road, hill,
mountain, stream, bridge. While in a trance, boredom van-
ishes, time is brought to heel.

Also not sleeping. I have never been an insomniac.
I have a peasant woman's constitution or at least I used
to. My soul goes to sleep at night and sometimes has bad
dreams but has never tossed and turned till dawn. Until
now. My legs move across the bed, searching for H. My
mind races toward him but he is not there. I think of trivial
things like where I put my sunglasses and whether or not
my granddaughter at age two and a half understands that
her grandfather cannot come to see her anymore. I take a
Tylenol. I take two. I do not sleep. A great roaring is in my
brain—it is as if I were trying to nap under the stars on the

veldt as an approaching lion pawed the ground beside me. I tell my doctor. He sends me away with a prescription for Ambien. It works. I sleep an untroubled sleep all night but three nights later I wake at four and am unable to return to sleep. And then I wake at two and then I increase the dose of Ambien and I sleep again and a few days later at a higher dose I wake after a few hours. I become obsessed with sleep. I spend the day avoiding my exhaustion, afraid to close my eyes in case I steal sleep from the nighttime hours. My doctor switches me to Lunesta. It works on night three but by night five it is less effective than hot milk, which really doesn't work no matter how many people vouch for its soporific powers. All I can talk about is sleep. Some weeks go by. I decide to go without any sleep medication, to recover my memory of what it was to sleep without fear of not sleeping. The first night without any Ambien at all I am up all night, and for five days afterwards I move like a zombie, sleepwalking in the daylight, haunting myself in the night. I go to a hypnotist who says he can help. I try his relaxation methods, thinking myself into a gentle place, but while I can calm my excited heart I cannot fall asleep.

And then finally I sleep again. I just sleep.

·   ·   ·

The shock has begun to wear off. I feel it recede. There are many hours of the day that I inhabit my own body, that I am not made of wood or stone. There are hours of the day when I talk on the phone with a friend and laugh at a story or absorb myself in the editorial pages of the paper just as if I were the same person I had always been. I turn off the lights at night. I am not uneasy in the dark. I rub my cat's head as I always did. He sleeps in H.'s place beside me. I am not surprised when I wake and find him there. For days after H.'s death he sat on H.'s side of the bed and let out a strange sound, a cat sound, a small repetitive shriek. I remember to go to the grocery store. I buy supplies. Without the shock I feel exposed, as if I were a mollusk without a shell, a formless thing, veins showing, trembling naked on a rock, a predator's next meal. My friends have all called and invited me to dinner. They have assured me that nothing has changed. They say it doesn't matter if we are nine for dinner instead of ten. But now the phone is not ringing and I realize that I must call, arrange things, plan to go to the theater with someone, suggest a movie, go out into the world on my own.

But if I am out on the street I want to be home. If I am at dinner with a friend I keep glancing at my watch, how soon can I leave, how long until I am back in my apartment. If I am in my apartment I am anxious. I should go out. I need to be out. I need to go somewhere. If I am downtown I worry about the subway on the way home. Will it come? Will I be safe? I go to the theater with friends. I want to leave at intermission. I can't concentrate. I am worried about how I am going to get home. If I am in my neighborhood I still worry. How many blocks away from my house am I? This anxiety, anxiety about nothing, no reason or sense to it, flows in and out of my mind all day. Did I lose my wallet? Did I leave someone waiting for me at a lunch I forgot? Do I have enough money in my bank account to pay my bills? Am I sick? Is my heart beating too fast? Will I have a stroke? Are my children unhappy? Do they need me?

When I was a child I went to a camp in Maine. In August on a clear night we would stay awake, singing songs and playing jacks on the bunk floor until the moon was high in the sky. Then we would put on our uniform blue sweaters and bring our scratchy wool blankets out to the flagpole, and slowly, as we leaned against each other, staring at the stars above and the moon making its way toward dawn, a pale light would appear at the northern end of the sky. It would grow higher and higher by the moment as we watched. It would now be tinged with pink and blue—or was it green?—and then perhaps purple as the lights shot up into the sky: Northern lights high above the pine trees. I was not frightened by the strange sky. I knew just where I was, on the damp ground of a camp by a lake in the woods. I was not afraid of the enormity of space or the smallness of my bones, although I was aware of both.

A counselor told us that the lights were the fingers of God, touching His creation. I was more impressed by the facts. Lights shone in my sky because in August the position of the moon was right, the stars in their constellations had moved, the weather was good, the North Pole was made of ice, white reflective ice. I understood that death was real and there would be no appeal when my time came. I did not know that it was someone else's death that would shatter me, leaving me afraid of lost wallets, loud noises, strangers in the street.

The last time I saw those lights was the summer before I was seventeen and left camp for the last time. Perhaps I could go to Maine and find them again.

And so I am alone. Not really all alone. My children are a phone call away. Friends are near and available if I need them. But I am mateless and that changes everything. I have always, all through our marriage, been a writer, a professional woman who might lunch with an editor, breakfast with an agent, have appointments to keep, a destiny of my own, separate from H.'s, separate from my children, a place in my head where I had my own thoughts and obligations. But I overestimated my independence. I now suspect it was never there at all.

When I'm alone without a destination, a friend to meet for lunch or dinner, the hours drag on. I know how to fill them. I could go to the gym and exercise. I could read a book if my concentration were better. I could invent a story or write an essay or clean my closet of unwanted clothes. I could go to a movie alone. I do none of these things. I hang suspended over my life. The phone rings. I come back into my body. I am interested again in the elections, in the grinding byways of Israeli politics, in the value of this or that commentary, TV series, theater. I hang up the phone and within a short time I have faded again. Is this the thing about being alone that I must get used to—I am not here if no one sees or hears me. Like the proverbial tree in the forest I neither fall nor stand unobserved. But I am observing myself and that should be enough.

It isn't.

There is a weight in my stomach as if I had swallowed a burned-out log: a taste of ash in my mouth.

H. returned home from his office around seven each evening. I would stand at my window on the fourteenth floor and watch him walking down the street. He wore his trench coat and an Irish wool cap in the winter. He walked fast. He was coming toward me. He would have his drink and we would talk. Not about his patients, that he would never do, although I would have listened. Instead we talked about our children, what worried them, what obstacles lay ahead. We talked in shorthand, whole paragraphs were left out but understood, whole pages quickly turned. We listened to the evening news. Then he would fix dinner. I stood at his elbow while he chopped or stirred. Now I don't know when it's time to eat. I don't know what to eat. The day has no appointed end. It drifts off into the night.

In my cabinet I have a huge bulging blue plastic file folder in which I put the condolence notes I received. The most valuable of these are the letters from former patients whose names I did not know, whose stories I will never know. One after another they spoke of how much H. had meant to them, how he changed their lives, made it possible for them to marry, to have children, to make good on days that had gone bad. They spoke of his smile, his way of listening, his caring, his way of noticing the smallest changes in their manner or look. One man wrote of the support H. gave him for his homosexuality in an era when other psychoanalysts were trying to change sexual wishes, erase sexual dreams, turn people into pretenses of themselves, carrying painful or shameful secrets that H. knew should be neither painful nor secret. One man wrote of his long-held hope that one day H. could be the best man at his wedding to his partner. There were dozens of photographs enclosed in these notes, snapshots of little children, families on a picnic, girls in ballet shoes, a boy with a bow and arrow and an older one seated at a piano, an adopted Chinese child smiles and waves to the camera. In one way or another each of the photos said, "Not without him." And now I am without him.

We had talked about this. He was born twelve years before I was. He was in good health and good mind but the possibility of widowhood haunted me. He said that it would be a compliment to our marriage, to his love for me and mine for him, if I managed this widowhood well and was able to enjoy my life with another partner or without. He expected that of me. He told me a dozen times in the last few years that I had made him happy. This was comforting but not comforting enough. The ash was still in my mouth. The log remained in my stomach. I considered that he had asked too much of me.

We had argued about the bedroom wallpaper. It had been on the walls when we moved into the apartment some eighteen years ago. The pattern was of repeated small bunches of flowers, blues and yellows, little touches of roses, and they were on a background of ivory and very dense, so that they seemed at a quick glance like a field full of wildflowers. This wallpaper spoke of New England inns and farmhouses in the plains. It was already dingy at the edges when we moved in. Increasingly the background turned to gray and there were peeling strips along the baseboard. I wanted to change the paper. H. wanted to leave it be. He was attached to it. He didn't want to spend the money. He liked it. He saw no reason for change.

I think of Charlotte Perkins Gilman's book *The Yellow Wallpaper*, written in 1899. A woman suffers from a terrible grief after giving birth to a daughter and is confined by her doctor to a bedroom with yellow wallpaper where she goes gradually mad until she kills herself. This novel is considered a primary feminist text. This is a story about how men impose literal and symbolic immobility. Here is a woman deprived of her own volition, chained to an infant, subservient to a husband and without hope. True, I said, dear Charlotte Perkins Gilman, true. I had been an early feminist. My mother had hobbled about on her Cuban heels while I had a first serve that whizzed past the boys. But I always had a tendency to wander from the political line. In the seventies I never considered that men were to blame for all oppression and I never believed that children were a burden. Mine sometimes were and sometimes were not.

I was raised, child of the forties, girl of the fifties, to flirt, to flatter, to flutter about. Those are traits that are hard to remove just because the climate changes. I admit to a desire, lifelong, to put my hand in a man's hand and let him lead me through the thicket of taxes and insurance and such. I want to go walking in the woods with a man pushing aside the heavier brush. I want a man to call a taxi or help me over a fence. I have always thought of men as the necessary other. The only question in my mind has been which man and when I married H. the question was answered. Still drifting, avoiding memories, sitting on my bed and not moving, finding it hard to go to the store and buy the barest of necessities, I was aware that in this widowhood I could use a sharp infusion of feminist pride, a sense of my own power, a disinterest in attachment, a venturesome soul daring to walk my own path. My first not-so-firm step was to remove the old wallpaper.

A painter comes. The wallpaper is stripped and gone and in its place a new lemon wall shines in the morning sun. I wish H. could see it. He would have liked it after all. Now

I have to decide if I am going to stay in this apartment or move, to a new city, to a little town, to a new apartment, near or further from my children and my friends. I make no decisions at all.

Except that I take an armful of H.'s suits and bring them down to my doorman to take to his church. I take H.'s old coats, the raincoat with its lining, the down jacket for weekends and country wear, and make a second trip. I don't think about each jacket, when he wore it last, the blue suit for the wedding of one of the daughters, the white suit for summer occasions, the heavy wool sweater worn to the office on cold winter days, I push away any images that dare to approach. I carry the clothes in my arms as if they were old newspapers. Then I am exhausted and fall asleep on the couch. I am not so sentimental that I would keep clothes in a closet that might warm another man on a bitter winter's night. I am not so intent on keeping the past in my closet that I would indulge my wish to keep everything just as it is. Nevertheless as I ride down the elevator with suspenders, shirts and tweed vests on my arm I feel robbed, absolutely robbed.

I remember the photographs of widows after World War Two, women in Florence and Sienna in black robes, with black scarves tied under their chins, with bent backs and heavy wool stockings, collecting wood or coal in baskets, or sweeping the steps or throwing buckets of muddy water into the streets. Today widows dress in their best clothes, wear all their jewelry and go out into the world to find a new mate, preferably one who can still drive at night. Will I join them? On the one hand I think it noble to attempt to regain what was torn away with the death of a partner, the sweetness of old love and the comfort of worn stories. On the other hand I may prefer to shut my door, play with my grandchildren, learn how to work my coffeemaker, also the Cuisinart, both jobs my husband considered his own.

. . .

A friend tells me that she has a friend whose widowed mother met a man at the 92nd Street Y senior club. They have been happily together for the last eight years. Of course, my friend adds, this mother is very beautifully dressed and is very careful with her appearance. I sometimes look like I slept in the woodpile behind the house. I live in an apartment, not a house, but all the same.

The moon pulls up as I watch it, from behind the apartment building on the east side of Broadway. It moves slowly into the center of my window and hangs there round, pocked, surrounded by space, black sky. A burst of smoke billows up and spreads out over the rooftops from a furnace in a building a few blocks away.

I was given by the funeral parlor several tall frosted glasses decorated with a blue star of David and containing memorial candles. I lit them. They burned for a week. At night I would sit in the dark and watch the light of the wick flicker back and forth. When they burned out I went back to the funeral parlor and asked for more. They gave me as many as I could carry. But when these burned out I put the glasses in the pantry cupboard on a shelf I can barely reach. Enough sentimentality.

What could be purer than death? There, not there. *Fort, da*, as Freud described a little boy throwing a ball under the bed and pulling it out again and again, attempting to

understand his mother's appearance and disappearance as
she moved through her day. Despite all the poetry and all
the melancholy sighs, death is simple, here, not here, not
returning. I wonder if everyone leaves a trail behind when
they go into the grave, a trail of resentment, financial knots,
undone, unresolved matters, lunatic ex-spouses, unreconciled children. No matter how fiercely loved the children
are, no matter how tenderly the relatives gather in a circle
around a table, things go wrong. When a family contains
stepchildren and divorced ex-spouses one always discovers
mold in unexpected places. My love for H. cannot alter
the fungal spread that stains our photo albums. The angels
accompanying him to the throne of heaven are playing
atonal music on their harps, although he loved Mozart and
deserves Mozart, an eternity of Mozart.

The discordance comes from a lawsuit. I cannot write
about why I am being sued for a considerable amount of
money stemming from something in my husband's past.
I cannot write about this or else I could be sued. I will
settle. My lawyer thinks I must. His brain is not unbal-
anced as mine may be. Nevertheless in my fantasy I take a
sailboat to the Cayman Islands and live outside the law, an
old gray-haired lady, browned and wrinkled, who arrives
each day to pick up books she has ordered from Amazon.
com. There at the sun-drenched dock by the turquoise
sea in which coral reefs shimmer as fish of every rainbow
color dash about, I will write postcards to those I have left
behind. I will befriend drunken sailors, ex-cons, fugitives
from white-collar investigations, and little children who
dive for pennies when the cruise ships arrive. Or not.

My lawyer calls. Do I have any secret bank accounts?

We went to psychoanalytic meetings in distant places. We spent summers by the beach, all the years of our marriage. We were content but the rugs were ragged, the house needed a new roof, the bills for crooked teeth were paid slowly and every once in a while the car insurance payment was late. We could have used a secret bank account. When my husband sent me flowers or brought out from his pocket a piece of costume jewelry he had found in a yard sale, there was always an accompanying card; it said, "From a Secret Admirer." That was our secret, our only secret.

·   ·   ·

Something about this book that I must say here. It is a well-known fact that when anthropologists study some isolated native tribe on an island in the middle of a distant ocean their very presence on the island alters what occurs to the people they are observing. There is no such thing as pure observation uncontaminated by the act of observing. I am writing this book as I am living my days but the act of writing adds a flavor, a possibly distorting factor to the story. Sometimes I have a thought while I am having my morning coffee at our local Starbucks and I decide I want to write that thought down. The fact that I have a purpose, that I have a plan, which is to write, changes the experience I am having in Starbucks. Writing this book provides a floor under my experience. Having used writing to hold myself erect all my adult life, I am bold enough to believe that I cannot fall because of this word scaffolding that, all invisible, props up my days. Perhaps I am wrong. Perhaps the fact of writing a book is not so life-saving as it seems. But it was necessary to acknowledge the fact of the book I am writing as I am living because without the book that I am writing which is the one that you are reading I would be a sorrier woman, a shell of a woman, lingering on.

THE MOON IS SHRINKING. IT IS THE SHAPE OF A FACE WITH a bulge on one cheek. Its color is faint. Clouds drift across it. It hangs above the sliver of the bridge I see in the distance out my bedroom window. The bridge has a small red light on one of its high points. I hear a dog barking on the street below, a deep and angry bark. I think of werewolves. If men can be turned into devouring wolves by the light of the moon, then women too can alter their shape. We can all become weretigers, werecats, werefrogs. Perhaps we do allow some beastly creature to emerge in our civilized breasts by the light of the moon. I feel tugging inside, a fury, a fury to slash, to harm, to run wild through the streets. I look in the mirror. I see only my familiar face. It is hubris to imagine the moon and its gravitational pull, its tidal forces, its mineral, gaseous, rocky back turned to our sun, would disturb the protein amino acid magnetic frictions of my human brain. But if I were a werewolf I would hunt down H.'s killer and rip him or her or it to bits. I would be ruthless, canny, foam at the corners of my mouth. I would do it. But a heart attack has no form, exists nowhere but in the arteries of its victim. I can neither slay it nor forgive it. I bite at my thumb as I do when I am angry: a bad habit.

. . .

I have an e-mail pal who lives in Fort Lauderdale. He sent me a letter in response to the personal ad in the *New York Review of Books*. We began a correspondence. He is a seventy-nine-year-old divorced ophthalmologist. He is retired and fighting a weight problem. His e-mails make me laugh. He's a tough, odd, curmudgeonly old bird, that he tells me himself. He grew up in an immigrant family in Buffalo and went to New York University. I understand where he came from and how hard it is to move in America away from the family of the first generation into the world at large. I'll call him L.D. He tells me that I should vacation in Florida and find a rich old man with a large paunch who will buy me baubles and such. I don't mind paunches but I have no interest in baubles. He tells me I should come to Florida and he would take me to the Everglades to see the alligators. He says he has no hair. I don't mind that he has no hair. He says he wants to leave Florida and live in a small town in New England and watch the leaves change color in October. He invites me to join him. I point out that we haven't even had dinner together. L. walks along the beach in the mornings. He reports on his diet and his lapses from his diet. He spends his mornings in the library reading. He is a fan of Elmore Leonard. After a while he sends me e-mails with group addresses. I become one of a gaggle of his female online friends. I like his grouchy manner but he is too far away for a real friendship. That requires a face and a hand and the sight of a broken tooth at the back of a smile. L.D., I send my regrets but we have to stop e-mailing.

. . .

The moon hovers over the water tower across the way. Low in the sky. It looks like a clown's teardrop. Tears are an interesting matter. I didn't flood with tears when we stood by the open grave. I was too shocked, too numb, and besides I wasn't sad, it seemed as if someone were operating on me and I was awake. I was without pain but without volition, without self. I didn't flood with tears at home when all the friends and family arrived with food and wine and concern. I was watching that no one felt left out, that strangers were introduced and could talk to each other. I was making sure that the platters of sandwiches and cookies appeared from the kitchen and fresh coffee was brewing and I was not crying. Sometimes when I read the condolence notes, especially from patients who had loved H., tears welled up, some escaped, but mostly they were denied, a shift of place, an opening of the cabinet for a glass, a phone call, they disappeared.

Before H. died tears used to erupt from my eyes at TV commercials with children running into their father's arms and dogs licking the hands of their owners. Tears used to flow at happy endings in movies and at sad endings at movies and many of my book pages are stained with tears. Tears apparently are easy when the situation that evokes them is pretend. Girls after all are allowed to cry even if it turns the nose red and the eyes become swollen. But when something shocking, real, happens it isn't so easy to let tears fall. H. used to say that women often cried when they were angry. I suspect he's right. But I am angry and I still don't cry. I also haven't torn my clothes or shaved my head or bayed at the moon. I understand those gestures belong to grief but they seem as alien as if I were to paint my body blue and dance stark naked down Fifth Avenue with bells on my toes. Tears seem to be unrelated to sorrow, at least my sorrow, which I feel like a weight in my chest, like a knot in my stomach, a dull pounding in my head. I wonder what other people's sorrow feels like. Is it like mine, evasive, boarded up, avoided, ready to burst out, curled up, hidden even to the self? Also as I feel tears appearing at the edges of my eyes I become afraid. Is it possible that I could dissolve in tears? The body is 90 percent water, they say. What if all the inner structures, all the sinews and arteries and brain tissue collapsed as I cried, what if I couldn't stop if I started? My task at the moment is not to float away, not to crumble or dry up or rot with water damage. My task is to manage.

·   ·   ·

My husband was a man consumed with his love for his children. I knew this before we married and had our own children. I could see it in his eyes when he looked at them. I could see it in his hands when he touched their heads. I could see it in his smile when he talked to them. He told me on our first date in great detail about buying his younger one a toy oven and how he kept it in his apartment for her when she visited because her mother would not let her take it home. We took children on our honeymoon. We were not always good parents. But we were always parents. That was the primary subject of our lives, even after the children grew up, even after we knew we had done well with some and not so well with others. We were only human, we told each other. We tried not to talk about our children all the time, hardly ever when we were with friends, but to each other we admitted our pride, our deep pride, our regrets, our mistakes. Our children were our fortune, our land, our nation. In other words we did what we could. We also knew our limitations. The children mourn him. Above all else he would have wanted to spare them that pain. I burn, fire rages in my brain when they speak to me of their memories, of their missing him. I listen quietly and nod, and sometimes add a few details to a memory that has faded over time. I am still a dutiful parent, the only one they have now.

· · ·

I am forwarded the psychoanalytic publications that once went to H.'s office. I read them from cover to cover. I memorize the names of new medications. I read about new theories of transference and countertransference. I understand everything but I have no use for the information. There is no psychoanalyst in this house anymore. I search for case histories. In them the patients are given initials. They report their dreams. They have trouble working or loving or both. I read their secrets the way one opens a fortune cookie at a Chinese restaurant. Perhaps I will find a message meant just for me. I wonder why I am reading. I keep the publications in a corner of the bedroom. I look at the covers and sometimes I think I should throw them all out. I don't.

· · ·

I am going to Broadway to purchase coffee and a roll. Now I know how to make coffee but I don't want to. Orange plastic ribbons run from one side of the street to the other.

Police barricades prevent passage. Several cars with red lights spinning on their hoods are at both ends of the block. Two fire trucks are parked along the way, firemen move back and forth, their black plastic coats, their yellow stripes, their big hats, their boots moving around and around. I see a huge tree that has fallen on the roof of a Budget truck that was double-parked on the other side of the street. The truck's roof is partially crushed. The tree's branches are askew, its thick trunk is bent way over as though bowing to some unseen royal being. No, I can't pass through. I walk around and go down another street.

That afternoon I walk to the corner. The street is cleared. No police, no fire trucks. I walk down the block toward Broadway and I see it, a huge chunk of sidewalk has heaved up and cracked down the center. The tree has been sawed off and all that remains is a circle of raw wood surrounded by a mound of dirt. I look at the rings in the wide stump. Its thick roots must have gone deep into the dirt and back underneath the brownstone buildings behind it. I stand there. I attempt to count the circles but I lose track. The tree may have been here before there were subways, before there were apartment buildings on Riverside Drive, maybe it was here when Henry Hudson sailed up the winding river not knowing where he was going or if he would return. How many wars ago did it root itself in the ground, how many babies in carriages rolled past it not noticing its height, its breadth, its breathing out oxygen into our air? It was gone in an instant. *Fort, da*, what made it heave up onto the sidewalk at just that moment? Two Hassidic Jews, one older than the other, in high black hats, white shirts, black jackets with the fringes of their tallith

hanging out over their pants, come down the block. They
are heavily bearded with bushy eyebrows and black shiny
shoes and pale faces, lavender shadows under their eyes.
They stop by the tree and take out cigarettes. They pull
out lighters, they smoke, inhaling deeply. I sit on the stoop
behind them and watch. One finishes his cigarette and
throws the still-lit end into the dirt by the tree. He grinds
it out with his black shoe.

How could such a tall tree fall? It was not called to God,
of that I am sure.

· · ·

The phone: "This is Susie of the (name blurred) national
polling institute. Can I speak to Dr. Roiphe on questions of
national importance?" "He can't come to the phone right
now," I say. Questions of national importance will have to
go unanswered.

· · ·

Once a long time ago we had a twelve-year-old daughter
who had pneumonia and recovered. But soon it became
clear that the pneumonia had left her with lung damage.
For months we watched as she ran fevers at the end of each
day and lost weight and coughed through the night, leaving
dark green spots on the wall by her bedside, which I would
wash off each morning. I thought of F. Scott Fitzgerald's
friends Sara and Gerald Murphy, who had lost a child to
tuberculosis. I thought of all the children who had died of
polio and ear infections in other centuries where the death
of a child was never a surprise. The doctors said that our
daughter would not survive unless they removed the con-

taminated part of her lung. Deep in its tendrils the bacteria had settled and no antibiotic had the power to penetrate through the tangled brambles of tissue. We went to the hospital the day before her surgery. In the room next to hers a small boy was dying of leukemia and his father was a policeman and the police bagpipe unit came to serenade the child. The sound was meant to cheer but it didn't. In another room a Hispanic family gathered around the bedside of a child with diabetes. At visiting hour the mother's pastor and ten congregants came to visit the child. They lit candles and threw rice around the room in ceremonial passion. The nurses came to forbid the candles and demanded that the crowd of visitors leave. The pastor continued his chants. The candles continued to flicker, their lights casting shadows on the curtain pulled around the child's bed. The nurses called security. The congregants blocked the nurses' entrance to the room and when the security guards arrived the congregants singing in Spanish threw rice at their heads. Everyone was shouting. My daughter put her blanket up over her head. The candles burned on. I took my daughter to the elevators planning to flee. Then it was over and the pastor finding us in the lounge offered to come and repeat the ceremony for my daughter. One congregant kindly threw a bowl of uncooked rice under my child's bed. I wanted H. but he couldn't come because he was home with our other daughter who was of course in need of his company.

H. and I waited in the cafeteria for the operation to be over. It was supposed to take two and a half hours. Five hours later the doctor had not emerged. I did not let go of H.'s hand. Something had gone wrong. "Don't imagine

anything," H. said. I nodded. But I was imagining everything. "I will die, if she dies," I said. H. let go of my hand.
"You will not," he said. "That is unacceptable," he said. "I
don't mean it," I said. "You can't threaten the universe," he
said. An hour later the operation was over. They brought
her down to the intensive care unit, tubes with blood running from her side, a tube down her throat, but her color
was pink. She was no longer the ashen green of her year
of illness. H. brought me a container of watery coffee.
We didn't have anything we needed to say to each other.
We just leaned one on another like people standing on the
roadside shocked to be alive after an accident that crushed
their car.

·   ·   ·

I feel a surge of envy when I see a woman about my age in
a restaurant with her spouse, the two of them talking softly.
Are they planning a vacation or worrying about their kids,
a job lost, a divorce, a setback of mind or body? Are they
talking about their friends, analyzing this or that foible, this
or that peculiarity? Are they talking about the abductions
in Baghdad or the CIA prisons hidden in byways of foreign
countries? Are they discussing his blood pressure medicine
or her next dental appointment?

I am becoming selfish. I can't remember other people's
birthdays. I forget to ask about their children. I am self-
absorbed. That is to say it takes all my energy to hold
myself together. This may be a normal response to a great
loss (I expect it is), but I do not like myself like this.

If I were a polar bear I would go into a cave and hiber-
nate.

We are, however, social creatures. The need for touch is built into our biology. If the first mother had not swept her baby up into her arms and folded it into her flesh and fed it and watched over it, the helpless baby would have died, and with it the entire human experiment. H. believed in Darwin the way hedge fund managers believe in the market. He said we need a group for protection, for efficient food production, for survival. We are not single predators, we are not fish that mate without touching. Right now I think I am more fish than mammal.

I watch television without caring if the victim is avenged, if the murderer is caught, if the good doctor gets the woman of his dreams, if the serial killer gives himself up. H. could fall asleep watching television. Perhaps the drama in his office was sufficient. I always had to wait until the plot's resolution. I had to sit through the commercials because I needed to know how the story ended. Now I don't care anymore. This is not good but I have no idea how to bring back my appetite for story, my connection to the people in my life. Perhaps time will restore me, perhaps it won't.

H. read every Trollope novel at least four times. He had his favorite heroines. Lady Glencora, Jane, Elizabeth. He was fond of the Pallisers one and all. When we married, his prize possession, not trusted to the movers but carried in his arms to our new home, was an old, brown-leather, yellow-paged 1894 edition of the Trollope novels that spread out across two bookshelves. He read and reread George Elliot. Sometimes when we were riding a distance in the car he would tell me the plot of *Daniel Deronda* in all its detail. It didn't matter to him that I knew the story, had read the

book. He liked telling it to me. I liked listening. Again
and again he read Patrick O'Brian's novels of the sea battles
between the French and the English. His favorite character, Doctor Maturin, was a spy, an adventurer, a sailor, to
whom he was particularly attached. If in my imagination I
bore a certain lifetime resemblance to Nancy Drew, then
he was Maturin, physician to the captain of the ship.

Born to immigrants in Brooklyn's Jewish neighborhood
of Flatbush, H. attended movies every Saturday afternoon,
where he learned to speak without the Yiddish inflection
of his parents or the Brooklyn accent of his neighbors. He
told me that at a Saturday matinee double feature in 1936
he won a raffle and brought home a box of brand-new
blue-and-white porcelain dishes to his mother.

It is amazing that the nineteenth-century world of English gentry could so hold his attention. He would not be
pleased at my current disaffection from stories. He would
be impatient with my wet mood. I assume he would understand that my mind is restricted in its play for good reasons.
But he would not want such a condition to become permanent.

·   ·   ·

I once had a long-widowed friend who said that she loved
her bed and her television and her kitchen and she felt well
only inside her apartment. I thought this was sad, I thought
that she had retreated too soon. But now I understand this
better. It is becoming true for me too. The familiar forms a
cocoon around me, asks nothing of me, provides me with a
space to let my mind roam where it will. I am less anxious
inside than out, less vulnerable, less apt to wonder what will

become of me. I understand that at a certain age there has been enough adventuring, enough sailing forth. It seems right to curl up like a sick cat on a pillow and wait for the end. I see this and I fear this.

"Yes," said Molly Bloom. "Yes," say I. If anyone asks. Although I have my doubts.

.   .   .

I go to a Sunday-night dinner—it's not just a dinner. For many years H. and I have gone to this house and watched the Giants football games with other fans and spouses. We have a betting pool. Each of us writes on a small card the name of the winner, and by how much. It costs ten dollars to enter. The cards sit in a large glass bowl in the center of the dining table. H., child of the Great Depression, hated to lose the ten dollars but was willing. Sometimes we held the dinner at our house. Often H. and I watched the Giants in our bedroom. He, covering his eyes when the other team threatened or walking out of the room if one of ours fouled or fumbled. H. reached for the sports section first thing in the morning. It was a lifelong habit. "Why would you read the sports section before the first page?" I asked. I never got an answer.

This time I go to watch the game without him.

Wives sometimes go into another room and talk or play Scrabble while the game goes on. Some wives leave after an hour. A few watch. I watch. I like the male talk about point spreads and injuries and weights and coaches' failures, and the quick reports of what has happened on the field before it is explained to the television audience. I listen when one or another of them gives the reason for

the red handkerchief tossed on the ground before the referee calls out to the stands. Sometimes the referee wearing
his prison-stripe uniform yells, "Unnecessary roughness."
As if the entire game weren't unnecessary roughness. I
like the male jostling in the room: which baseball player
hit the most home runs in 1974? Someone will know. Are
there enough Jewish players in all baseball history to make
a team? And then they start to name them. Such and such
a player had a fractured tibia four years ago and hasn't been
the same since. They seem like a pack of dogs playing in
the yard, yelping and nuzzling, a smell of wet fur in the air,
licking and jumping. Without H. there I feel awkward. But
then I don't.

What I wait for is the moment when the quarterback
swings back his arm and hurls the ball halfway down the
field and his receiver, outrunning by a half a step his pur-
suer, puts his hands in the air and pulls down the ball, as
if it was always meant to be in his arms, as if it was cho-
reographed that way, and the crowd cheers and I feel for a
moment as if anything is possible. Strange that large men
can commit such acts of God-like grace.

I lose the football pool. I, like H., bet out of loyalty,
not sense. The odds are always against me. There was a
purity and an absoluteness in H.'s attachment to his teams.
His heart could be broken by a dropped pass, a stumble at
a crucial moment, a kick that fell short of the goal posts.
This drama is the way some men play with fate. Sitting
in the room before the television set, nibbling on cookies, I think of H. Not sadly. Not with pain. I just think
of him. Love wells up from far within, the way the whale
breaks, the spout shooting upwards, the smooth surface of

the waves splinter into foam, the dorsal fin rises across the surface of the water. Glorious—even if the image is used in a TV ad for life insurance.

·   ·   ·

I see a play about a woman dying of breast cancer. Her life ends when one character whispers in her ear the best joke in the world, a joke so funny that the listener laughs to death. The conceit is both charming and grating. Would that death were so easy. I have thought about it. The window, pills, the ocean, the gas stove—I hold the idea in my mind, saving it for the right moment the way one might a good champagne, a piece of jewelry reserved for such a special occasion that it hasn't yet arrived. Not right now. My children would grieve. I would not want to cause them pain. They should not have to lose two parents within a short time span. Aged orphans they will one day be but they should have time to get used to the idea. I am loathe to leave the story before its end, although I suppose I will in time, just not now. I still have friends I want to meet, movies I haven't yet seen, books to read that might not even have been written yet. Old age with its dribble and tremble and watery eyes and half-hearing ears is not a delightful prospect, but erasure can only promise itself. The choice remains mine. I'll take it when I'm ready. I won't need a joke, especially when the joke's on me.

·   ·   ·

A man calls me. He is a widower. He lives in Brooklyn. He is an acquaintance of a friend of mine. He is a doctor. His wife died five years ago of a long and terrible illness.

He invites me to lunch on Sunday. He is an ear doctor who
is still practicing a few days a week. He has just purchased
a condominium in Sarasota and plans to spend ten days a
month in Florida. I agree to meet him on Sunday. I begin to
imagine myself in Florida reading a book by a pool. I think
of the warm sun on my legs. I know about the malls and
the golf games and the early-bird dinners but I am thinking
of blue water and red flowers and palm trees. I am thinking of a man's razor in my bathroom. I think that maybe I
could slip myself into another life. Maybe. Sunday comes
and I dress carefully, my best sweater, my new skirt. I look
in the mirror, not too long. I am about to put on my coat
when the phone rings. It is my lunch date. The tunnel to
Manhattan has been closed for repair and he cannot make it
into Manhattan. He'll call another time. I go for a walk on
Broadway. I am not going to Florida after all.

•   •   •

I had not imagined all the legal forms that follow the death
of a spouse. Death certificates—tax papers, conversations
with lawyers and accountants. I wander in a deep wood
and I am way past the middle of my life. Have I made a
major costly mistake, here or there or everywhere? Money
is just money and I have not paid as much attention to it as
I should have. This is my error. I tend to wait for rescue by
a shining knight. Not this time.

I HAVE BEEN GOING TO CONCERTS WITH A MAN I'LL CALL M. I had known him when he was the partner of a woman I knew. They stopped seeing each other a few years ago. A friend of mine who knew him said she would call him and find out if he had a new lady friend. "Thank you," I said. She told M. that I was widowed. She told him I would be pleased if he called and he did. M. is a retired divorce lawyer. He is also a pianist. Music is now his main passion. He has tickets to opera and tickets to concerts and a gadget that lets him hear any opera he wants on the nearest radio: a sweet soul this. He is a tall man with a softness to his body, but he walks fast, holds my arm tight. Not only is he fond of divas but he is also a baseball fan. He takes me to the Yankees game. He has me meet him in front of the stadium. He tells me what subway to take to get there. I walk with the crowd to the gate where he will be waiting. The crowds flow past. If H. were with me I would hold his hand tightly. I would not want him to lose me in this river of fans. The sky is a light blue and the lights on the stadium cast a yellow color across the faces of those approaching the ticket-takers. No reason to be alarmed, I tell myself. I know how to find my way back to my home. M. appears with tickets in hand. On a folded piece of paper on his lap he keeps track of every action on the field and marks down errors, successes, scores. We take the subway back to Manhattan and he tells me what stop to get out to take a bus to reach my apartment. He stays on the subway.

I wave good-bye to him through the window as the train pulls out of the station.

Another night, after a Mets game, he takes me back to his apartment. It is small and cluttered with file boxes, old articles, notes, other people's papers, the boxes rise toward the ceiling. Shelves are filled with CDs. The television is programmed so that the classical music channel plays all the time. The television is never turned off. To move to the kitchen one has to thread through the boxes around the piano. I see photos on his kitchen wall. He names his children for me. He tells me their occupations and what worried him about one of them and what pleases him about another. He asks me nothing at all. I ask him about his law partners. He answers directly. I ask him about his childhood and he tells me: the grief of losing a father, the shame of poverty, the pride of the school he attended on scholarship. He speaks of the religion of his childhood and why he left it. I ask more questions and still more questions. He does not ask me anything at all. I ask him where he likes to travel, where he has been that he returns to. He tells me. He still asks me nothing at all. Imagining that he might be too shy to inquire about my life, I tell him what comes to mind. He is not paying attention. I stop. He walks me to the subway and tells me what train to take to get home to my house.

Several concerts, four baseball games later, at my apartment I go to bed with M. Sitting near him, his hand on my shoulder, the leaning in, it happens, without my willing it, or not willing it. I thought it time. I thought I needed to know if the man was there under his clothes, behind the music he listened to, behind the commentators' voices of all the baseball games he had watched and recorded on his TV. I thought the sweetness of him might carry me through. I thought I needed to know that my body can go with another body again. I was glad to go to bed with M. My shape was no longer a wonder to behold. Neither was his. My heart was beating fast, my desires rose. I was able to give and receive. But how strange it is to be in bed with a man who is not H. Am I betraying H.? I had never done so. I had declined invitations to lunch, an opportunity here or there while I was away on speaking trips, a psychoanalyst colleague of H.'s who sent me notes tucked into books he thought I might like. You cannot betray a man who is not living. I tell myself this. I firmly tell myself this. On the other hand you can betray the memory of the touch, the muscle of the legs, the mole in the center of the back, the slightly curved spine, the way the hair curled at the nape of the neck. You can betray the indentation of the man you had been in bed with night after night, good nights, bad nights, dull nights, year in and year out. Perhaps this is why in bed with M. I start to feel like a mannequin, a person who is there in this space but not there. This is not M.'s fault. He is tender. He is sweet. He is strong. I respond, or my body responds as it should. This is good but not good enough. My mind remains outside, above, away. I watch myself do things that seem normal but are not. I do not inhabit my body. Perhaps I need more time and distance. Perhaps I really am betraying H., although he would not think that, or would he think that—and just not tell me? My cat circles around the man, an arch in his back, a sound not entirely friendly coming from his cat throat. M. rests his head on

the pillow that now belongs to the cat. I reach across M.
to run my hand over the cat's ears.

There is the idea in my head of the merry widow. I am
not merry.

·   ·   ·

I can't hang a picture on my own. I can't open a tightly
closed jar. I can't work the clasp on my pearl necklace. I
can't get it open and if I get it open I can't get it closed. Or
can I?

I invite M. to the beach for a weekend. He talks politics
with my friends. He listens to music. He does not like the
sea. He does not want to walk about. His life is interior.
The sun gives him a rash. But we are peaceful together. All
around are photographs of my children and grandchildren.
He doesn't notice. So I pick up a photo of my two granddaughters and tell him their names. He turns his head away
and does not look at the photo. It is true that other people's
grandchildren are superbly uninteresting. They are just
children after all and the world has its fill of them. The
special charge, the electric joy these pictures give a parent
or a grandparent disappears when the eyes are colder, less
kind. But most of us are polite enough not to turn our
heads away when presented with a photo obviously dear
to the presenter. I am feeling lonely in the house with M.
I fix dinner. We eat and talk over the editorials of the day,
the failings of the newspapers. He tells me stories of legal
battles he has fought. He talks of lawyers who are so fabled
ordinary people know their names. He does not ask about
my work. He has read nothing of mine. A book I wrote,
a memoir that I gave him when we first started dating, sits

unopened on his shelf. I try not to be hurt. Why should he read my book after all?

He says, when I inquire, that he is not a literary man and worries that I will not respect his thoughts. But I am not a lawyer and I don't worry that I should be. Is he insecure or just telling me an approximate truth, an untruth? I tell him he has expressed no interest in who I am. "Maybe," he says. But still he asks me nothing.

When he packs to leave I am not sorry. I welcome back my solitude. Either I am not ready to place my hand in a different hand or this man has circled his wagons against the irritations of another soul, at least my soul. I will not see him again. He is decent and good and intelligent. He is calm and self-contained. He e-mails me, "Perhaps we could be friends?" I don't answer the e-mail. He is a stranger and will remain so.

It occurs to me that I could write anything about him I like. He will not read it.

Sometimes at the end of the day I would read aloud to H. the page or two I had written a few hours earlier. He would sit on our black leather couch with his vodka in his hand and nod when he was ready for me to begin. He was mostly appreciative and always encouraging, except when he fell asleep. This happened often enough in the last years that I stopped reading to him. He rose before six and was gone by seven thirty a.m. He walked the twenty blocks to his office. He carried with him the book he was reading. I knew his mind was full of his own thoughts and mine must have served like the lullaby wheels of a train, round and round, clank and churn, clank and churn. H. had earned the right to fall asleep as I read. Also I might have been boring (all writers fear that they are boring, a violation of the first of the writer's ten commandments). I was not afraid that H. would leave me because I was boring him.

This is the first summer since we bought the house that I have not wanted to walk along the water's edge, watching the ocean come and go, watching the gulls circling for bait fish, watching the trawlers out at the edge of the horizon. For reasons I do not understand I am uninterested in the beach. I am unable to sit in a chair under an umbrella peacefully. I do not admire the little children who run about. I do not want to hear anyone else's radio. I get cold with the sharp wind. I get bitten by black flies. Also I do not want to be alone on the beach, not even when the fog comes in and the terns scurry on their pin legs, in and out of the tidal froth. It's too much for me, this ocean. I never go. Day after day I plan to go but I don't. As if I had signed a pledge, do not enjoy, do not let the sun near the muscles of your back, do not wet your feet. Ridiculous. Perhaps I act this way because the house is going to be sold. Widow that I am, its upkeep will undo me. Widow that I am, I have no desire to travel the highways to reach the house. Widow that I am, I do not want to put my hands in the rocky dirt of my garden. I don't want to replace a burned-out lightbulb. I don't like this house without H.

But that said, it is also true that here we had Thanksgiving dinners, a Passover or two, with most all the children gathered. Here we played poker with boyfriends of my daughters who seemed permanent but weren't. Here we talked about politics with a young husband who disappointed and disappeared. Here another daughter brought her new husband whom we had not yet met. On this table, with this stove, and this refrigerator marred by specks of rust on the door, common to houses so close to the sea, we made meal after meal. We cooked together, all of us. A daughter announced her pregnancy here. Another was married nearby. Friends filled the house, fish was smoked and grilled. Bikes were pulled out of the shed and stuffed back in among unused boogie boards and mildewed beach chairs, grandchildren slept in baskets, on couches, Scrabble pieces fell under the table, cookie crumbs were ground into the rug. Wet bathing suits hung on the shower pole, mice were in the cereal boxes, insects in the bag of flour. Also fights. This sister complains about that sister. This sister weeps for her dog who died. This sister feels ignored by the others. This boyfriend goes off on a bike ride and disappears for a full day. This is the place where one daughter and her husband decided we didn't want them to stay longer in the house and became angry with us. This is where we brought one daughter home after an eye operation. This is the house where one daughter wept on learning that another was pregnant. This is the house that was invaded by rabid raccoons who jumped about inside the walls, a terrible stench filled two rooms until they were trapped, caught in steel jaws that left them lying open-mouthed, bloody, bones, fur, guts spilling, on our porch.

I no longer wanted the house. It was ungrateful of me. The tightness in my chest was not the house's fault, although the blame must fall somewhere.

I have a strange virus. I have not had such a fever since long before I met H. Now this ache in the limbs, the rise

in temperature, the need to sleep, the muscle cramps last
and last. I am tested for Lyme disease. I don't have it. I go
by jitney to my doctor in New York. My liver is inflamed.
My potassium level has sunk to an unacceptable low. I give
more blood for more tests. The unnamed virus remains
with me. I am alternately hot or cold. I try to go to a party
but my head swims. I leave the party. I try to read but
the lines dance on the page. If H. were here I would be
coddled, calmed. He would make carrot-ginger soup. Am
I sick because he is not here? They say that the immune
system responds to crisis by shrinking. Has my immune
system turned from plum to prune in the season since H.
died? I know that everything is not a matter of psychology.
On the other hand the body is not separate from the mind
and this mind feels as if an ax has cleaved it in two. No
wonder I have a virus.

After three weeks it does depart. I never learn the name
of my tormentor. It would cost one thousand dollars, my
doctor explains, to find its name. I am not that interested.
I think of Adam in the first week of the world naming
the animals as they walk past him. Was there also a parade
of bacteria and viruses and other microscopic life forms
crawling across the grass of Eden so that Adam could grant
them their identity? I know I am fortunate—I could have
been invaded by a million worse diseases, ones that might
have consumed me altogether. But I am not grateful. The
absence of H. seems, like an oncoming tide, to be covering
more and more of my being with each passing day. Run,
run to high ground, I tell myself.

I'm invited to swim in a friend's pool. I don't want to
swim. I don't know why. I am a good swimmer but now I

dislike the idea. Why move my arms and legs about just to get from one side of the pool to the other? Why bother?

I think of other summers I have had that were less than perfect. In August, when I was three, my brother was brought home from the hospital. August has never been my favorite month. Once in August in the time of my first marriage I was alone in the city with my young child. My first husband was gone for good and the slightest sound could make me jump. I had dreams of falling objects, closet doors that wouldn't open, cliché and bathos followed me everywhere. My friends were away. There was a heat wave that could kill. I sat at an outdoor table in a nearby coffee shop, sweat dripping down my peasant blouse, and chain-smoked Camel cigarettes while my child rode her tricycle around in circles by my feet.

I have trouble reading. I am an escape artist who reads newspapers, books, cereal boxes. But now my concentration is cracked. Stray thoughts disturb my peace. The bird song on the nearby tree makes me close the covers of my book. This bird has an unlovely voice, his call is loud and grating but his mate appears from the other side of the garden and sits on the branch nearby. Evolution has programmed her to admire his voice. H.'s voice when he spoke to patients was gentle and soothing. You could lean on that voice, you could depend on that voice. It was a big voice although he was not a big man. Under the words lay a melody, a promising harmony.

People come from time to time to see the house, potential buyers. When they come I leave and go sit in my car in the parking lot near the beach. I inhale the salt smell. I watch the mothers carrying wet and sandy children in their arms. I note their buckets and shovels and towels and flip-flops and beach chairs. I see the teenagers flirting with each other near the ice cream truck. I let my arm hang out the window and later I see that my elbow has turned red. The tip of my ear is also burned.

No one makes an offer. The market is bad, there are fourteen houses for sale within a four-block radius. I worry I won't be able to sell the house. I worry I will be able to sell the house. I worry that I will lose my friends who live nearby. I will lose some of them. But I know from experience that with change other people will cross my path, other people with stories and bad habits and children who do or do not bring them pride.

The broker comes and goes and replaces his sign with a larger one. We are at the end of a dead-end street. No one sees his sign. The days are gold and the light is warm and silken. I should sit on the patio at my table where the umbrella with a print of roses going round will protect me from skin cancer while I watch the bees swarm and the black crows hang in the branches above. But I don't go into the garden. Instead I sit on my bed. I wait until a decent hour to call my daughters. I also tell myself old stories. I embroider them with slight untruths. I wallow. This is unacceptable.

A friend asks me, "Are you used to your new status yet?" What does this mean? I would check the box that says widow if presented a form at a doctor's office or the Department of Motor Vehicles. I no longer have a joint bank account. The joint is gone. I have changed our credit cards into my name. But status? Could it be true that a woman without a man is always at the edge of appearing as a figure of fun, a disappointed person like a nun or the obese girl who stays home the night of the senior prom?

There are millions of women who live alone in America. Some of them are widows. Some of them are divorced and between connections, some of them are odd, loners who prefer to keep their habits undisturbed. They like the way they keep their cupboards, feed their dogs, stretch out on the couch, wash the ring off the tub, put the coffee cup in the dishwasher, always on the left, handle-side out. Never mind the howl of country music's unrequited love, someone stamping around after midnight, lots of people are unmated and comfortable, feel no need to swoon into a microphone. Someone in a marriage must die first and many people live in single space peacefully.

But how do they do it?

I go to a luncheon. The guests stand on the lawn, glasses in hand, gazing down at three egrets who stand each poised on one leg at the water's edge. I am introduced to a widow of some five years. "It's horrid," she says, "and it's going to get worse. They don't know, they with their husbands, they don't know." I nod. I know about some other horrid things too, that have nothing to do with losing a spouse, things that hover about the garden casting shadows here and there despite the high sun and the perfect weather.

·   ·   ·

A builder over the last two years has been constructing a huge house behind ours. Now it towers over my house. It looms above my red maple tree. The workers' voices rise across the property line. I hear saws, hammers, small backhoes dipping their steel jaws into the dirt, trees falling down, the radio with its loud unreal conversations, music you can't dance to, on and on. The house they are building is grand. There is a giant pool and a little pool house that abuts my now-leaning fence. Four big brick chimneys rise to the sky. There is a deck but little grass. Where will the buyers put their garden? I hear from my neighbor on the other side that the builder has sold the house. I hear that the buyers are from Colorado and are in oil or gas and have business interests in Russia. I hear from the man who cuts my grass that the new owners have bought the house to the left of them and have put in a bid for the house to the right of them.

And then they come to see my house. I am out. They come twice and they bring an architect and I whisper into my cell phone: They're here again. Will they notice all the windows that do not close and the stain on the kitchen tiles that I can't scrub off and the drainpipe that is crooked and the broken screen that the cat has scratched, through which mosquitoes and spiders arrive and depart? I meet her. She is a young woman from Texas. "How did you ever get so many books?" she asks. "My husband liked the house because of the books." "I'll leave them for you," I say. At last they make an offer. They will have a family compound. They will have a little estate. They will have closed a circle. Now they will have grass and a Japanese red maple tree that turns orange in August and all my blue hydrangea bushes. They are not, they say, going to tear down my house, just fix it up, a new kitchen and new bathrooms and new closets and new floors and new wings and surveyors come and engineers come and I am ready to go back to the city and let the house go but I am aware that this sale is an amputation, a necessary amputation. Another one.

Now I have another lawyer. He is a real estate lawyer who has drawn up the contracts for the sale of our house at the beach. I would like to keep it as a place for the family to gather at holidays. I would like to keep it because I love the small stone statue of a child that H. bought at a yard sale and the morning light transparent on the grass. I love the pink blossoms on the dogwood tree that come just as winter fades. Then there is fog and the sea and the clams at the clam bar and I love my friends who invite me to dinner and worry that I am too alone. I am too alone.

But I cannot keep this house at the beach. Sometimes here at the beach I fear that I might die in my sleep and lie undiscovered for days.

I cannot keep this house because I cannot afford it.

This lawsuit pursues me, I need to be careful with funds, to protect myself from becoming destitute in my frail old age. I am not overly concerned. I have no enormous desire, no secret plan to live long years in an expensive nursing home, requiring help to boil an egg, someone to bring me medicines to calm my raging mind. I suppose it is a moral failure, this lack of appetite for life on my part, life of any quality. I admire those who grab it all, want every moment, fight cancer with every tortuous new treatment imagined, travel to the far ends of the earth pushing their walkers, tasting all foods as they arrive at the table, demanding more and more. I am simply not like that. I am too much of a realist to battle against the odds. Or I am a quitter.

Today there are people wandering through the house.

They are picking up dishes and thumbing through our books and looking at the paintings. We are having a yard sale, my daughters and I are here, watching the strangers. The tables and chairs are being carried away and the canister I bought at a yard sale is being recycled to a plump man in a yellow shirt with golf balls on it. Someone wants my duvet and someone else wants the painted cabinet with roosters on the panels.

I am fond of my things, my accumulated things. The ceramic fish that rests on the table near the model ship, the wooden crane that has one blue eye and one black, the espresso cups from a trip we took to Portugal, the drawing of Jean Marais done by Jean Cocteau. But I am not so fond of them that I will not let them go. Like memories that are lost in the far recesses of the brain, like days that are swept away unremarked or unrecorded, I am willing to let objects leave with their new owners. This house must go and I will close the door on it with regret but without anguish.

What is the point of anguish? Certainly material things do not deserve a drama of their own. It is the unseen, still lingering, presence of the man who lived in this house with me that takes my breath away. My head swims. I need to sit down as someone takes the dollhouse we kept for our granddaughters and walks through the door.

If I were a cartoon character I would have stars circling my head and Xs for eyes. Actually I deserve a medal for bravery—or is my bravery foolishness or is foolishness the explanation of bravery? I find an old hairbrush behind a bureau—so that's where it went.

H. loved his drawings and he loved his paintings and he

hung them on the walls with great care and he was always convinced he'd purchased a treasure, something of real value. He loved the seventeenth-century Italians and the sixteenth-century Dutch and he loved paintings of women with curves and drapery and enigmatic smiles. I loved his loving his drawings. I myself lack a collector's will, a joy of possession. It is a flaw of mine, not my only one. Standing outside the now nearly bare house, surrounded by my daughters and their daughters, and packing the car for our final departure, I look at the bare walls for the last time.

The drive back to the city takes forever because of the traffic. My daughter K. is with me. Her child sleeps in her car seat. Her head is tucked against the side. The child will not remember her grandfather although she will have photographs of him. There he is holding her a few hours after her birth. There he is with her mother and aunt and there he is holding a fish, a large fish, smiling with such pride you might think he had created the fish, not merely reeled it in. My friends have grandchildren. Sheepishly we show each other photos. It makes us feel like clichés to do this. We feel like characters in an old *New Yorker* cartoon, matrons with hats and wide hips who belong to garden clubs, not working women with titles of our own. Nevertheless we want to show each other our grandchildren. Is this the point after all? Will I live to see this child become a teenager? Will this child remember me when she has children of her own? H. would say that doesn't matter. Don't ask for more than you can get. Enjoy the sleeping child in her apple juice—stained shirt, clutching her precious blanket. Appreciate that she is not complaining about the length of the trip or the lack of amusements in the car, or the fact that we have no more boxes of apple juice.

I do not dream about the house. Sometimes I think about the ocean, walking along the ocean's edge. Sometimes I think of the dunes. I remember the jellyfish floating in the waves. I remember the fishing boats with their huge nets rolled around the gears at the horizon's edge. All this is permanent and returns summer after summer. The haze in the morning, the fog that rolls in from the North Atlantic sea, the driftwood blanched white, the abandoned balloons from a child's birthday party, the bed of broken clam shells, the tiny stones with blue veins, the gulls with their grating caw, the half-buried red plastic pail, the ruins of a sand castle, return. I was the visitor, the one passing through. It's time to go. H. would not complain that biology is biology, that beginnings have endings, that doors open and then they close.

•   •   •

I have lost weight. Enough so that my wedding band slips up and down on my finger. I play with it with my thumb. I turn it around and around. It is a simple gold band. I have worn it since we were married. I think I remember taking it off in the hospital when I gave birth to K. and B., or did the nurse put adhesive tape around it? You would think after all these years that it would have grown into my skin. It has not. I slip it off. I put it back on. I go out to dinner without it but rush home and put it back on.

The American Psychoanalytic Society always had its mid-winter meetings in New York, at the Waldorf-Astoria Hotel. The red carpets shone. The candelabra were golden, the staircases marble, the mirrors reflecting the tinsel-and-red ribbons of the Christmas season, and in the lobby psychoanalysts and their wives came and went, off to lectures, to symposia, to meetings on transference, transgender, techniques, termination, etc. In the hall outside the meeting rooms a long table sat lined with books written by the analysts in attendance or their colleagues long dead. Stacks of papers that were being delivered during the day were available for perusal. It seemed as if we were on a ship, Transatlantic, glittering in the air, sealed off from the traffic outside, from the concerns of others. Older famous analysts stopped to visit with their younger students and analysts remained students and supervisees for many years. It was a long apprenticeship to become an analyst, filled with ambivalent loves, secrets spoken, dissected, repeated, in rooms with volumes of Freud lining the walls, little statues of far-off civilizations sitting on desks, Oriental rugs on the floor. Secrets that meant that the older analysts knew the darkest thoughts of the youngest and the youngest yearned for the attention of the oldest. Some, who believe that psychoanalysis is a dead profession, may think that the ship we were on was the *Titanic* but to me it seemed like the inner chamber of the heart, the essential organ.

My five-year-old daughter, E., went to the movies with her babysitter and I went downtown to the Waldorf to meet H. We were going to buy the ring, the ring for our marriage, the ring I would wear ever after until death did us part. I rushed into the lobby. The uniformed doormen, who seemed both martial and like extras in an opera, stepped away to let me pass. I looked up the marble steps and saw H. coming down toward me. He was carrying a briefcase. His winter coat was swung open. He would not kiss me in public, not before his colleagues, not on the steps of the Waldorf lobby but when we emerged and walked to Madison Avenue on the way to the jewelry store, in the privacy afforded by the crowd, he did and I was safe, moored to this man. I pressed against his arm. I, thirty years old, believed that nothing was impossible.

On my fifth or sixth or eighth attempt I take the ring off and keep it off. I look at it in its box. I hold it in my hand but I do not replace it on my finger. I am not married anymore. I have no mate. I cannot keep twisting and turning that ring on my finger.

H. did most all the food shopping. He liked picking and choosing among the fruits and vegetables. He liked choosing the fish or the meat for the meal. He dawdled in the aisles checking prices and he read food magazines for recipes he clipped and would make on rainy Saturday afternoons while one ball game or another played on the television. Now that he is gone I have discovered that I am the world's worst shopper. I buy things I think I want to eat and then they sit in my refrigerator ignored until green mold appears, when I throw them out. I buy too much milk and have no cereal. I buy a can of soup and forget it in the cabinet. I buy pasta that turns stale. I spend too much money. I buy paper towels by the dozens. It will take two of my lifetimes to use them all.

I resort to takeout food; the Cuban-Chinese restaurant on Broadway will deliver, so will the Mexican place a block away, and the Indian and the Turkish cafés around the corner. I overtip the man who comes to the door with a bag containing my dinner. "Make yourself a salad," my daughter K. says. But I don't want to. "Do you want to come for dinner?" my daughter B. asks. But she lives a forty-five-minute subway ride away. She is a law professor and comes home tired to her husband and baby and more often than not they eat takeout food too.

The thing about takeout food is that when it is removed from the kitchen of its origin it loses its balance. It becomes all curry or cumin or soy. Its colors fade like a flower picked in the field, pale before you are back on the path. A smell of paper carton or plastic wrap sinks into the sauce. Now I have enough takeout menus in my drawers to paper a room. My taste buds are complaining. All these Mexican, Indian, Chinese, Turkish, Cuban deliverymen carrying my dinner to me, waiting at the door for my tip, they know my name, they smile at me, they wave good-bye as they wait at the elevator. It is not a sign of normal life when the takeout deliverymen become fond of you or your tips.

I do go to dinner at my stepdaughter J.'s home. She lives only ten blocks away. The family gathers around the table and the children talk about their violin lessons, their science projects, their rehearsals for the class play, college applications, debate societies. I listen and I see clearly that their home is a good place, just as it should be. I am welcome but irrelevant to the evening, like an extra waiting in the wings for the crowd scene. In this apartment there are no photographs of me. That is because the biological mother comes to dine, and will sit in the seat I am now in. Perhaps that's why I lean back in my chair as if I were a ghost not fully visible. Of course I often turn into a shadow. I speak but am not speaking. I see but don't record what I see. Here in

[am safe, protected by this family, and a curious
rings up in me. I look around the table. Mine,
y dearest, without the word but with a heat that
might bring tears if I allowed it. I don't.

• • •

There is the problem of H.'s ties. For the eighteen years we
lived together in this apartment they were on a tie rack on
the inner door of my closet. Each time I opened the closet
door they swung outwards. Each time I closed the closet
door one or two would get caught and protrude into the
hall. I would have to open the door and put the ties back
in place. I give one away to this friend and another to a
son-in-law and one to J.'s oldest child who is going off to
college but many are left swinging on the rack, sticking in
the door.

I take them all off and intend to give them away to a
thrift shop. The pile lies on my bed, formerly our bed. I
leave them there. At night I toss them on a chair. In the
dark they look like vines crawling. In the morning I put
them back on my bed. An hour or so later I take them
carefully one by one and return them to the rack. I do
not want to give them up, not yet. The same is true of the
two-dollar bills that H. kept in an old wallet in his drawer.
A patient has paid him in cash, all two-dollar bills, several
months' worth of sessions. He was amused. He said it was
all right. He left me hundreds of dollars' worth of two-
dollar bills. I could use them. I could go to the bank and
deposit them. I keep them in the drawer. Two-dollar bills
are lucky, they say. Despite all evidence to the contrary,
they, like the ties, stay.

Here is a difficulty I have not yet solved. The world outside my brain is as always in a woeful state. I am aware of genocide in Darfur, of women with dead babies in their arms, of refugees wandering barefoot in the dirt. I know that car bombs and snipers' bullets and assassins who drill holes in their captives' heads are not figments of my imagination and I know, and this is very personal, that Israel has blundered in Lebanon and that threats to its people abound. I know that need is everywhere and that if one listens carefully in the night air a pitiable sound rises to the stars. And my solitary state is hardly newsworthy, comment-worthy, significant in such a context. I know that the disruption and destruction of my life is neither tragedy nor pathos. But, and here is the rub, we do not live in the general mind, we abide in the details of our private stories. Mine matters to me and I have trouble staying at such a distance from myself that I can worry more about the orphans in Ethiopia than I do about who will have dinner with me tomorrow evening.

I have no right to complain. I complain.

I have an old friend whom I love despite or perhaps because of her unvarnished style. She calls to say, "I wouldn't want to be in your shoes." I understand this is a perfectly reasonable thing to say. I wouldn't want to be in my shoes either if my feet had a choice. Nevertheless her comment rankles. Not because I would wish widowhood on her but because I feel diminished. I feel pitied, which is unpleasant. I hear her finding herself superior, which while fair enough, makes me cringe. Was there a better way for her to say that? "I understand how you must feel" might have been kinder but less accurate. "I'm so glad my hus-

band lives while yours is moldering in the grave" would
be accurate but even less polite. You would never say to a
friend, "I'm so glad I'm not driving a Saturn like you, my
Lexus is such a wonder." You might think such a thing of
course but you wouldn't let the words escape your mouth.
But the rawness of death, the jaggedness of this loss, as if
a thunderbolt had split the tree on the lawn in two, this
brought out the comment "I wouldn't want to be you."
Who would?

* * *

I have taken to reading the travel and real estate sections
of the paper with an unnerving zeal. I look at each picture of a house overlooking a lake or a mountain and I
think maybe. Maybe Colorado with its wildflowers and red
rocks, or maybe South Florida, where I see an affordable
condominium with a view of the ocean and a terrace with a
lounge chair. The sky is perfect blue and the ocean stretches
as far as the eye can see. Then I see a gray-shingled house
with a porch on an island in Maine. Could I live on an island in Maine? Maine has high pine trees, cones lie on the
dirt paths. The steeples of churches announce the towns
as you approach. There is a barrenness to Maine that stirs
me. There is the lack of fresh paint on the walls of the local store. There are the dark long lakes and the mists that
take forever to lift and the cold mornings even in August
and the northern lights. I have always imagined myself in
Maine. But now? Then there are photos of apartments in
Tel Aviv, ones that look down on the beach, ones that are
near the busy markets. I don't speak the language except in
my dreams when sometimes I hear myself in fluent Hebrew.

I have no friends of my age there. I have nothing now to offer the country, except the trouble of burying me. The moment for the move to Israel came and went without my stirring. It is hard to move away. I see a photo of a small house on Lake Tahoe. I would like to be in a small house on Lake Tahoe. I would have a big dog, maybe two, a pickup truck. I would go to the local library and read and read. I would wear a squash-blossom necklace and turquoise bracelets on my arms. But I don't know a soul, not within two thousand miles. The question is would I meet people? Would I? What if a widower lived down the road and came over to help me stack my firewood and what if we cared for each other? And what if no widower lived in the entire state and I sat by the phone waiting for my children to call? What if I found a senior citizens' community and moved there? What if I missed all I have here and wanted to return and could not?

The fantasy of a new life plays in my head. It goes round and round, until it is stopped by a wall of reality. If I were twenty I would go. If I were twenty I would not hesitate.

I might hesitate. After all I'm still here in the same city that raised me. I have not seen the world. Well, thank God for movies. Sundays I read the travel section. Perhaps I should move to an island in Hawaii. Perhaps to New Zealand. Perhaps I should volunteer in an African refugee camp. If only I were a doctor or a nurse or even a teacher. They do not need writers in refugee camps.

I remember the time at the beach house we played poker by candlelight when the hurricane came. I remember H. standing in the driveway with a plastic bag filled with blue fish with their heads still on and their tails pressed against each other and the smell of sea and fish on his clothes and in his hair. I remember my stepdaughter nursing her baby on the couch. And then I forget.

What I want, really want, is my old life, in my same place, with H. by my side. All the rest is flight.

*   *   *

I am contacted by a man who knows my cousin. He is an engineer who has his own business consulting on automation. I see his photo. He has a warm face with a short white beard. He lives in Pittsburgh, which is very far from New York City. He is from Belgium and when we speak on the phone I hear an accent that makes me think of cobblestones and archways and cypress trees and sidewalk cafés. He tells me that he has been divorced for a long time. We talk about his work. I tell him about mine. He tells me that he would take me to walk the mountain trails near his home. He tells me that he likes to dance and would take me on a boat on a lake. He tells me that he is ready to love a woman with all his heart. I am touched. He sends me a long love poem he has written. It is atrocious. It is worse than a greeting card. I pause. I think that if I were to write anything at all about a mechanical object, a scientific subject, the construction of a bridge, it would be terrible too. I would write gibberish, so perhaps I should ignore the poem. I do. We go on talking. He tells me about his great car, a giant SUV that he uses to travel across the country in his consulting work. He tells me that he invented a kind of robot now used in manufacturing. I am impressed. We agree to keep talking. He sends me the pages of a romance novel he is writing online. I cannot read them. I explain to him that I read different kinds of books. He accepts that. We talk about meeting. I could take a train and we could meet halfway between his home and mine. I like his voice. I have grown used to hearing his message on my machine.

Then he tells me he will come into New York City and spend the day with me. He sends me his train schedule. He will arrive early in the morning and I will meet him at the station. I am pleased. I am a little excited. I think of walking in the woods. I think of the steel mills by the river. I think it doesn't matter that he is a Lutheran and I am Jewish. Those distinctions belong to another time of life. He promises to tell me about his divorce when he sees me. He says he will explain the mistakes of his life. I will have to explain my own mistakes as well. I am prepared.

But then he says that his life was changed by Dr. Phil. I don't respond. The conversation ends. I think about Dr. Phil. He has changed many people for the better, I am sure.

But I am of a different sort. Dr. Phil is like a leech on a fevered brow. I know he is popular. I just don't belong with a man whose life was changed by Dr. Phil. I call Pittsburgh and explain that I can't meet him at the train station. I have had second thoughts. My fault, I say. I am not ready, I say. I am still grieving, I apologize. I don't say anything about Dr. Phil.

Then I wonder: Am I being small-minded? Am I cutting off a possibility because I am afraid of the new and the different? Am I just playing with the idea of a new life with no intentions of really claiming one? Perhaps I should ask Dr. Phil.

•   •   •

I remember the night we went to hear Anna Freud speak.
The event was at an auditorium at a city college. She was
small and dressed in black, with white hair. There were no
empty seats. Psychoanalysts of all kinds had come to hear
her, to applaud and to feel themselves close to the source, to
pay their respects. This was before all the attacks on Freud.
This was before it became clear to everyone that psychoanalysis was too expensive, would aid, if it would aid, only
a very selected few. Psychoanalysts were pushed off their
pedestals. Nevertheless I was a member of that community.
I knew what they were talking about, jargon and all.

A friend sends me an e-mail. It has a single name on it.
I call her to ask why she sent me that name. "I heard from
my sister-in-law, the divorced one—that this B. is a man
to stay away from. If someone introduces you to him, stay
away from him." My friend tells me that he's been widowed for about three years. He's a psychoanalyst. Why had
my friend sent me his name? To warn me, she said, she
was afraid I would be introduced to him since we had so
many connections in common. I am intrigued. I Google
him. I find the address of his office. I write him a note. I
introduce myself. I suggest that we might enjoy meeting
each other. What am I doing? This is not the way women
of my generation behave. It is unseemly. It is also absurd. I
have just been warned the man is no good and so I go rush
toward him as if I wanted nothing more in the world than
a no-good man. I drop my letter off at the post office.

The very next morning the phone rings. This is Dr. B.,
the voice says on the phone. He has a low, calm, reassuring
voice. He liked my note. He is intrigued. He wants me to
meet him at the Harvard Club the following evening for

dinner. He will meet me in the lobby. I agree. All day I walk around holding his name in my mind. I think, perhaps, perhaps, perhaps. I remind myself not to anticipate more than a dinner. But all day the possibility of Dr. B. runs like a shiver down my spine.

It is raining the next night. I dress carefully. I put on shoes with heels and a gold buckle. I don't care if my toes soak in puddles. I arrive at the Harvard Club and there he is sitting in a chair in the lobby reading a newspaper. He has a strong face, a head of silver hair, a warm handshake. We go into the club, the mahogany dark club, with its maleness everywhere and a certain sad look to the chandeliers as if time had passed it by. Its solemnity now hollow, like an inn in the mountains that has lost its clientele. We talk, Dr. B. and I. Perhaps I talk too much. He asks me how I heard about him. I tell him. Was this a mistake? I want to interest him. I ask him questions. I find out what there is to find out about a psychoanalyst, a doctor who is used to not answering. He went to Harvard. I know his kind. We talk about our children. Perhaps I talk too much. Perhaps not. Then he walks me to the door of the Harvard Club. He lives on the East Side. I live on the West. The rain is coming down in torrents. He says he is going away for a week on a trip with one of his granddaughters but will call me when he returns. I walk off in the rain, my umbrella over my head.

The next morning he calls before eight o'clock. "Who is the person your friend knew? Who is the source of the warning about me?" That name I had not told him. I didn't want to tell him. I was embarrassed at my lack of tact. I had not been sworn to secrecy but still the entire conversa-

tion was indiscreet. But I gave him the name: a woman I
didn't know. He said to me again, "I will call you as soon
as I return."

But he didn't call, not the next week or the week after.
He didn't break my heart. One dinner, a few hours' conversation cannot do that. But I tasted disappointment. Yes,
if I leave my house for encounters with strange men, rejec-
tion is a possibility, a likelihood, a certainty some of the
time. This one I deserved. It does not startle me that I am
not universally loved by all who have dinner with me. I am
a writer and know that bad reviews are as likely as good
ones. In my imagination I had already begun a time when
this stranger and I would go to the movies together and
more. But in this case my imagination misled me. Little
harm was done, little grief will be spent on the matter. It
was not meant to be. Nevertheless for the next month I
worried the matter. Was it my age, my conversation, my
manner? Had my flirtation skills grown rusty? Was I so
used to being loved that I assumed the whole world would
love me if I wished? And then that was that. Some weeks
later I tell the story of the meeting with Dr. B. to an analyst friend of mine. She tells me that he had been brought
up on charges before the medical society because he slept
with a patient. This is not exactly akin to being an ax murderer but it repels and disgusts nevertheless. What luck he
never called me back.

·   ·   ·

If I could keep my children from ever finding out that I
had lifted my hand against myself, I would. They stand in
my way.

. . .

H. believed what he believed. He did for his patients what
he could. He knew that Freud, error-filled or not, had been
among the first, artists aside, to explore the underground
river of the human mind, where the unacceptable thought
floated and the less lovely, more feral creatures lurked on
slimy rocks. Freud was the one who told us that we were
far more than our conscious minds, our sweetest selves are
but a sham.

Which is how it happened that one morning I woke
thinking of the ways that H. was less than perfect. We say
only good things about the dead. A eulogy is a mud pie of
compliments, of perhaps exaggerated compliments. A good
eulogy makes the mourners feel uplifted. But eulogies do
not serve as portraits of the dead. I need to be accurate.

H. always frightened me while driving and we drove
the highways almost every weekend out to the beach and
back; a trip that would take a normal driver close to three
hours was often for us less than two and that's because H.
liked to be the front car in the pack. That's because he drove
fast and moved incessantly from lane to lane and nothing
I could say would stop him. I had long ago decided that I
would die in a car accident with him one day and accepted
wordlessly all the swooping and the veering and the close
calls. Still it made me angry sitting next to him that he
indulged his racing-car fantasy, his World War One pilot
fantasy, in the car with me, with the innocent cat in the
backseat in his box, and some time on this earth still ahead
of us. Yes, he was right, he did not die in a car accident and
he did not harm me. He had driven over sixty years and no

one was ever injured (a few cars were scratched or bent). But as a driver, behind the wheel, he was unkind.

He was not good at psychoanalytic politics and did not dodge and weave among the psychoanalytic entities that made careers for psychoanalysts. He did not follow any orthodox line altogether. He worked with infants, observing them with their mothers; he had original ideas and published original papers but he could not befriend those he did not like and he could not pretend to be accommodating. He was not. This is a virtue and a fault. He knew that about himself. He understood himself. It would have been better had he been a more worldly man. He would have enjoyed more of the honors his profession dispensed.

He did not believe in interfering in his children's lives. They have to make their own decisions, he would say again and again, which sounds virtuous but sometimes made him seem an absence when he should have been a presence and sometimes stemmed from a desire to avoid controversy. He slept soundly on nights that I tossed and turned waiting for a child to return home, waiting for news of one sort or another.

Sometimes he was too silent. Sometimes when he was angry or upset he pulled into himself like a turtle and the shell was impenetrable. I had to wait, to coax him out, beg him to return. He would get angry while paying the bills, including his lifelong alimony to the wife he married first but shouldn't have. He would sit soundlessly for hours at our desk with the papers spread before him. A more perfect man might have left me a life insurance policy. He had a policy for his first wife, which he was legally obligated to keep for years, and after that he was older and the policy would have been costly and we never quite had the extra funds. I understand but the idea stays in my mind. He should have protected me. It comes to me that a more perfect man would not have left me to send out death certificates. He also protested when I wanted one more child. Just one more. I didn't insist. We had enough. He was right, we couldn't afford it. But still I wanted another baby. A trace of anger burns across my brain.

But the worst thing he ever did was to die.

H. always did our taxes. He pored over the statements from the bank, credit card bills, and would list all possible deductions. He had folders and papers and a system repeated year after year. When all was done I signed the returns and mailed them. I have held tax papers in my hands but never looked at them. My eyes are virginal. Now I try to imitate old notes. Now I try to find out what he was looking for in the credit card bills. Now I am the sole taxpayer, the citizen, the one who should remember and mark down expenses and charitable contributions. My mind rebels. It is not just. It is not right. I was not made for numerical matters. This is his job. But he is not here and now I will do it, badly, but I will do it. Resentfully I will do it.

Psychoanalysis is an art as well as a science. Everyone says that. H. knew that. Still he wanted to be a scientist. He wanted to see if the child did indeed develop as the textbooks say, in the real world. That's why he spent years observing mothers and their babies in nurseries at major hospitals. He, with a colleague, directed the nursery. He advised the mothers. He held the babies. He was in love with both infant and mother, with the bond that rose between them. He wrote down the ways a child could separate from its mother, how it ran toward and away, how its body reacted in fear to the mother leaving the room. He was an expert on infant sleep troubles and eating troubles and slow speech and he ran a nursery for troubled infants who had no physical disability but were not speaking or walking, whose eyes wandered about aimlessly. He worked with a staff to restore the crucial human connections, to bring these fragile babies back to life. He talked about how children react to the differences between the sexes and how it made boys and girls behave differently. This was a dangerous conversation in the early feminist years. He didn't care. He saw what he saw and published it in papers. When he talked to me about what happened in his nursery, when he explained to me his ideas on anger or shyness in small children, his voice would grow even deeper and I was held as in a spell by a great wizard, a wizard who was my spouse.

·   ·   ·

A friend, not the first to do so, suggests I dye my hair. She says, "It will make you look younger." It would. I should. Maybe I will. I don't want to. If I were to do it, the color of my choice would be purple, punk purple, magenta purple, or perhaps I could get black and white stripes like a skunk. If I have not met a man to cherish for the remaining years, it cannot be because of the color of my hair, or can it?

·   ·   ·

Through the glass windowpane I see a man eating dinner alone. He has gray hair and a book on the table beside him. Why are we both alone? I see a man walking past the greengrocer with a cane and a cap on his head like the cap H. used to wear. The man is alone. I walk a little faster so I can see if he is wearing a ring. He isn't. But that is not conclusive. He might be married. He might not. You can't stop strangers on the street and ask them if they are married and if not would they like to stop for a cup of coffee. Too bad.

I receive a notice from the cemetery. I need to order a headstone. I need to send them money to dig the foundation for the headstone. I need to approve the words put on the headstone. I had asked H. if he wanted to be buried or cremated, a long time ago. He said he didn't care. It would be up to me. I asked him why he didn't care. He shrugged. It would make no difference to him. He was not one to follow religious traditions. On the other hand he would be perfectly respectful of anyone's desire to do so. Cremation saves space on this earth for the living, which highly recommends it. On the other hand Jews have been buried under the ground forever, believing—some of them—in the coming of the Messiah and the resurrection of the dead. I have no desire to visit a grave site. I have no illusions that I would be closer to him there than in front of my television or on my block, or standing on my subway platform. I do think that when I watch a Giants football game, I am nearer his spirit than when I lie limp on my couch, not thinking anything at all, but letting time wash over me, waiting for the day to end. But this kind of nearness is not literal, nor corporeal, nor in fact very convincing at all.

I decided to bury him in the ground because I thought it better for our family, because traditions are ignored at one's peril, later they might seem important. This choice of mine is expensive. H. would hate the expense. I feel guilty. Is this wasted money? Of course it is, but done.

It is winter now. A mild winter but still no time for visiting headstones. We will go in the spring. I purchased two plots. One now used, the other for me. This will save my children anxiety. This will put my remains beside his—not that either of us will ever acknowledge the other.

I think of the ground that was dug by the employees of Mt. Eden cemetery—I see the small backhoe, the darkness of the earth. I am not afraid of death. I have no expectations of heaven or hell or judgment to come. But something chills me in the thought of him, no longer him, changing shape, losing tissue and sinew and becoming all skull, all bone, there below in the ground where I can't touch him and he can't touch me.

I see the decay. I see how little remains. I push the images away. They return. I see a hand, an eye socket, a bone. I don't want to see this. I don't have a choice. The images come now and then, prompted by what? I do not know. Is this a result of guilt? If it is guilt is it Eve's guilt or some personal spasm of conscience? Is it the result of a lifelong bad habit of burrowing in the sore spots? I do not for a moment think it is H. I am seeing. I am expecting no rising, no bone rattling, no hauntings. Alas poor Yorick. I think it is Yorick I am seeing.

·   ·   ·

Perhaps I should have had him cremated after all and spread his ashes on the sea where he had gone fishing for blues summer after summer within sight of the Montauk lighthouse. But there seems something ridiculous about saying the Kaddish, the prayer for the dead, over the huge dark sea, even near the harbor. The prayer for the dead is a list of praises for the Lord and H. would have protested, why didn't God take an extra day or two to create the world? He might have done a better job, he would say. He would especially have protested at his own unasked-for death. But we did say the Kaddish at the grave site and he would not have minded. Do what suits you, he had said when I asked years ago. I find the words of the Kaddish comforting, the rhythm of the prayer comforting, because it is ancient, it links us together in time. It is a prayer against despair because it is said aloud with one's fellow humans. I don't fool myself. This grave site is not for H. The ceremony that accompanied the body down its hole was not for H. It and the bill were for me.

I finally go to a movie alone. I choose my movie carefully. I choose one that H. would have wanted to see: the new James Bond. H. could watch James Bond movies over and over again. He was never bored by them, never found them silly, improbable, nonsense. All things I said at least to myself. Still I had enjoyed them, because H. was laughing, gasping, holding my hand. Now I go alone. The plot is not much, the beautiful girl beautiful, the exotic scenery exotic and the evil ones very evil. It seems strange to be sitting alone in the movie theater. I feel self-conscious. Of course no one is looking at me, not even when the lights were on, before the previews started. The ticket taker didn't say, "What are you doing here alone, lady?" The young couple the row behind me didn't whisper to each other, "Hope I don't end up like that." I recognize

that the whisper is my own. Ten minutes into the movie I
forget that I am sitting next to strangers on either side, and
I am inside the film. James Bond is talking to me. That is
the way with movies. I leave the theater with the throng
of people arriving and departing all around me. I am glad
I went to the movies. I can go alone whenever I want.

I REALLY WISH I COULD WRITE ABOUT THIS LAWSUIT. I CAN only tell you that someone H. was obligated to now wants a piece of him, because of legal agreements forty-three years old, agreements signed long before I met H. and we married and made our life together. I can only tell you that the lawsuit went into mediation. My lawyers met with other lawyers with a judge who helps both sides negotiate an agreement. This is better than going to court. It is better than a long expensive fight. It means that I sit for hours on a bench in a glass office building in the middle of a distant suburb while in a room across the empty hall on the other side of a bank of elevators, the lawyers are fighting. Across the parking lot I see a Pizza Hut and a Toyota dealership. The floors are marble, the elevators rise and fall, bells ring. I sit with my son-in-law, who is kind enough to keep me company but surely has better things to do. Nothing seems to be happening. I am not able to eat or drink. I think how H. would shrink inside himself if he knew this was happening. He doesn't.

I see my adversary exiting a door on the other side of the room in which I am now sitting, heading out for some air. I think unkind things. I would tell you what they were but I can't because I might accidentally identify my adversary. Another lawsuit would follow. A rank odor of loneliness and chronic irritation follows this person about. Once I did feel love for the human being that is now turning away from me. Once I had hoped we would be friends for life. I was naive. I had thought simple goodwill could overcome the tornadoes of emotion that blow across family histories. I had ignored the lessons of Greek tragedy and old fairy tales and assumed that all would be well. I was mining the mountain for gold with a teaspoon. If I were a better person perhaps I could recapture the love that once I felt. I am not.

Some people use money to gain what they feel they were denied. Such people use the court system again and again to exact revenge. I know such people are more to be pitied than to be blamed but that is less true when you are the object of their legal endeavors. I have little pity here.

After five and one half hours the matter is settled. My lawyers have done brilliantly. Her lawyer will take much of her profit. Nobody's life will change at all. I sign the papers in the lobby. I am tired, very tired. But the settlement is not nearly as huge as I had feared. In the settlement is a clause that protects me from further suits on this matter. My enemy cannot renew the attack. Relief floods through me. I want to kiss someone, my lawyer actually.

It's only money. But it's money H. had saved, worked for and wanted for his family. I have lost some of it, a small, tolerable amount of it. I can forget this now. But I won't, not entirely.

It seems odd to me in a book about the loss of H. that I should be writing about money at all. I am not Edith Wharton. I am not Charles Dickens or F. Scott Fitzgerald. Money and real human loss should have nothing to do with each other and perhaps that would be true if H. and I had lived out our lives on a kibbutz growing tomatoes, appreciating the wonders of drip irrigation, but here in America money is not a vulgar subject or rather it is a vulgar subject but one we must indulge, admit into our most private moments, lie about: how much we want it, how much we need, where we got it, how we value it. We respect the self-made but envy the inheritance of others. Money is dirty but lack of money is filthy. It is not happiness. Money has nothing to do with happiness. But it does affect everything else. I think these things in the car on the way back to the city after the mediation. I think what a wonderful novel about money I could write if only I wouldn't be sued if I wrote it.

This lawsuit has hung over my life, a cloud, a fearful haunting, for months now. It has frightened me irrationally. It has reopened a scar over which I keen. All the children and my friends will now pretend this never happened. Everyone knows who was on what side and what lies beneath polite smiles.

I go to a luncheon party. I see an old friend, a law professor. He walks slowly and with a cane and cannot stand for long. He tells me he misses H. because H. would always

come over to him and sit with him and they would joke,
their old, repeated jokes. He says most people do not join
him on a couch but leave him alone. H. would make sure
he had his drink. This conversation now brings a heaviness
in my chest and then a rapid rising of tears. Quickly I ask
my friend about the coming election, his expectations, his
opinions. The subject changes, the flow of my tears reverses
its direction. The heaviness in my chest remains.

•   •   •

I read in the class notes of my high school bulletin of a
widow who was contacted by an old boyfriend from college who had read her husband's obituary in the paper. She
met him and they rekindled their young love and are now
happily together in the college town where he is a professor.
I have heard several stories like this. Do I have any old boyfriends who might be available? I have a first husband but
he must be as unsuitable now as he was then and besides he
married a much younger woman so he isn't a widower. I try
to remember. I can't think of anyone. Bad luck I suppose.

I have a smallish skin cancer on the side of my face
beside my right eye. I ignored it for a while. It bled a little.
I went to the doctor, who sent me to a surgeon in the hospital to have it removed. They take it off, send it to a lab
while you wait, and if the margins of their sample do not
come clean, they take off some more, until they have it all:
cancer vanquished. I could have a plastic surgeon standing
by. I am not worried about a scar in a place a few wisps
of hair would cover. I am not worried about my life itself
because I have been assured such skin cancers are not threat-
ening. The doctor scolds about the sun. Ah the sun that I

have played in since I was a child, all the summers at the beach chasing waves in and out, all the summers at camp throwing balls as the heat caused sweat to run down my shirt. Ah the sun in the park where I watched my children climb and dig and put sticky fingers around melting ice creams. This is the same star that burned my face and gave me blisters when I was twelve and my mother and I stayed at a hotel in Miami Beach while she decided whether or not to divorce my father. She didn't: a mistake. The doctor is talking about the same source of radiation that melts the tension out of my back when I spend a few days in Aruba or Puerto Rico, that sun is the one the doctor, a pale man with no sign of ever having worn sandals to cross the hot sand, regards the way I would an alligator in my bathtub.

H. would have gone with me to the surgeon at the hospital. He would have complained about having to cancel patients. I would have said, "I don't need you. I can go alone." He would have said, "No. I'm going with you." Now I go alone. I sit for an hour in a crowded waiting room. Other people with bandages on their faces, arms, legs are waiting. Someone seems to be with each of them: a wife, a husband, a sister. I read the paper. I read the *New Republic* from cover to cover. Finally I am taken. The procedure is painless. I think about the umbrella we sat under at the beach and how I meant to stay in the shade but always slid outside into the warming sun. I tried to remember the brand names of the sunblock I had used. I always meant to reapply it after swimming. I usually forgot. The umbrella, the creams, the dark glasses I always removed immediately and placed on top of my head had always seemed to me impositions, restrictions on my freedom, prissy items. I wanted to be on the beach with my hair blowing wild and the sun beating down and my feet in the spray. This skin cancer was the price I paid.

I waited in the waiting room. I went downstairs to the hospital cafeteria and had a roll and coffee. I had a bandage on the side of my head. The cafeteria walls were painted a bilious green. The linoleum tabletops had long ago lost their luster. At the next table three doctors discussed their boats, which were each in need of repair. The plastic tray was brown and cracked. The long halls through the hospital, the silent people in the elevators, the ring of the cash register in the cafeteria, alarmed me.

I called my daughter in another borough and she offered to come and wait with me. I accepted her offer with some shame. Was it not my role to be with her when time was holding still, not the other way around? She took nearly an hour to reach the hospital and find me. When she did I was restored. I talk with her about her work, about her child, about the new coat she wants to buy. I see her reflection in the glass window. I look only at her.

The surgeon needed to slice some more skin from the wound. At last I am called to the operating room. My daughter waits outside. It is done. We wait together another two and a half hours before the report comes that all is well. The surgeon will sew me up soon. My daughter leaves.

What I know is that this is not the end of my hospital visits. Odds are very high that I will be waiting alone in rooms like this again and again in the years that remain. I do not have H. to stand near me.

•   •   •

There is a widow who lives in my building. She is considerably older than I am. A pile of yellow-stained white hair rests on her head. She wears a large-brimmed straw hat in all weather. Her back is bent over at a forty-five-degree angle. She wears long, flowered dresses over a short, shapeless body, and black boots. She has a wide jaw and milky-blue eyes. She pushes a shopping cart, which also serves as a walker. There is a sign on the cart that says, IMPEACH BUSH. I see her coming and going. I should do more than nod and smile when I pass her. I should speak. But I don't. She is like a storybook widow, perhaps a good witch. I, however, still look like most of the other people walking by. I don't send off vibrations of misery, or addiction or bizarre thoughts. I am not rummaging through the garbage cans looking for redeemable bottles or items that can be sold on a blanket in front of the grocery store. I think I still look gainfully employed, ordinary, as if someone is at home waiting for me. Actually I think I should make some effort to get in touch with my inner witch. Perhaps this pretense at normalcy is weakening my immune system, tying up my brains, and fooling no one.

I go to lunch with another widow in my neighborhood. She has been widowed for over twenty years. She is a fund-raiser for a major hospital. We talk in the elevator about her exotic trips, safaris and visits to Nepal and boat rides to the South Pole. She has a bright smile. She tells me that she is finally ready to meet someone after all these years. For many years she preferred to be alone but now she has worked through the problems in her own therapy and is ready to be with another man. She has found someone through an online dating service but he wants her to pay for her own dinner. This disturbs her. After twenty years of widowhood I think I would be glad to buy the man his steak and *pommes frites*. But perhaps not. I am sure that I would not have lasted twenty years alone. I have already located the window in my fourteenth-floor apartment that would be the right one to open and lean out, too far, irrevocably too far. I have chosen a window on the alley behind the building so that there would be no chance I could fall on anyone, also I chose a window where the resulting mess of blood and bone would be seen by as few as possible. I have already considered this carefully. Would I take pills ahead of time to still the pain on impact? How many pills? The plan is not yet complete. It is a plan I hope not to execute, at least not for a while, but it comforts me to hold it in my mind. I am reassured that I do not have to live beyond my desire to live. H. said that the best way to end your life is in a closed garage with the car motor going. But I don't have a garage. Perhaps the fund-raiser widow has never had that kind of dark thought, perhaps she is content with her life

I have lunch with the widow of a psychoanalyst, a colleague of H.'s, a woman I have known reasonably well. She is at least a decade older than I am. She was a refugee from Nazi Prague, hidden by nuns in a convent in Czechoslovakia. She was a beautiful young woman and is still a beautiful woman with dark, sad, distrustful eyes. I have hardly seen her since her husband died several years ago. This was careless of me, not deliberate. I feel guilty because I should have called her more often. I had not been a good friend. I don't deserve her friendship now.

Now she tells me that she never cooks dinner anymore.

She is glad not to be cooking. She eats her main meal at lunch and then sits with a snack in front of the television in the evening. She tells me that her children and grand-children visit but they make a huge mess, they make a lot of noise and it is too much for her, this rushing about. She has stopped making dinners for the religious holidays, which had once formed the center of her family life. She belongs to a book club that meets once a month. She has a friend she has traveled with every summer for a few weeks. She still works a few days a week as a volunteer at the library where once she had held a job. She has a respect-able life, but I can tell from her tone, from the flatness in her eyes, that although she is doing all she can, she is listless. She lives dutifully but not brilliantly, as a prisoner adjusted to their prison might do. She tells me that many of her and her husband's friends stopped inviting her to dinner within a year of his death. This is the cruelty of the social world.

I ask her if she is having trouble sleeping. "No," she says. "I sleep too much. I sleep usually ten hours at night and then a few hours in the afternoon and sometimes I doze in the morning. I have trouble staying awake." She knows as I know that sleeping this much is a symptom of depression. "What would I do, with the extra waking hours?" she asks. I don't have an answer. Suddenly I am not only afraid of not sleeping. I am also afraid of sleep-ing too much. There is no point in practicing being dead. There is also no point in staying awake just to convince yourself that you are not dead.

I have lunch with a good friend who tells me to join a club where writers go to have lunch at a long table and talk to one another. I say I will but I don't. I don't want to have lunch with strangers. I can barely manage to have lunch with friends.

H. wanted me to exercise three times a week so now I join a club. I try to go regularly. But one morning I am too exhausted from lack of sleep, another I forget completely, and then I have a cold or a meeting or a book to read. I will exercise when I can. Not now.

There is another widow in my neighborhood. Her husband was a principal of a school. She has not found anyone in the eighteen years since he died. We have coffee in her living room. If I press my face against her window I can see the bridge that spans the river to the west of us. I can see the black barge that sits in the river surrounded by ice blocks, stilled. She tells me that the man I saw her with on Broadway the other day, the broad-shouldered, mustached man, is a married lover of hers who was supposed to leave his wife but had just changed his mind. For a while we talk about men, their propensity for infidelity. We drink cup after cup of coffee. There is a sisterhood in the condition of widowhood but it has its limits. I want to hear good things about her life. She has none to tell me.

Over the years she has been with other men and when I passed her on the street or stood with her at the corner she would blush a sweet pink color when she introduced me to this one or that one. She is a woman who has a goodness of soul, the kind that any child could recognize. And even she has not found a connection to a new man or contentment without one. She had not been ready to lose her husband, they had so many years ahead of them. Still I would have thought that she would by now have been in someone's arms. "Being single sucks," she says. Her words frighten me without surprising me. Of course it sucks but shouldn't there be an end to it, when a widow can live happily ever after on her own? If life is a cabaret shouldn't there always be another act, at least until there isn't?

· · ·

I go to meet V. at the information booth of Grand Central Station. I have no idea what he looks like. He has written to me after reading the personal ad in the *New York Review of Books*. He lives in a suburb. He is a widower. He is interested in reading and is taking courses in the classical world at his local university where he has become president of its senior citizen organization devoted to aiding the institution. He was a banker. He writes that he retired early because his wife had rheumatoid arthritis and was no longer able to drive but she wanted to keep working. She loved her days as a dietician and so he stayed home to take her to work. This touches me. Here is a man who loved his wife and acted on his love. This is good. This man does not lack a soul. I call him. At the very least he will not harm me.

Years ago when I was young I met young men by the clock at the Biltmore Hotel. They were coming to New York from Yale and Harvard and Amherst and Dartmouth and they were shining with possibility. We went drinking at the local clubs. We went to hear jazz. I kissed them good-night. I played at falling in love. I loved the parade of them, the smell of them, the scarves they gave me with their school colors. I liked it when they stared at my breasts and pretended not to. But now I am at the information booth and the commuters are swirling around and the ceil-

ing of the railroad station is so high that it makes me dizzy
to look up at the glass dome and I feel ridiculous. He is
late. I am early. I am anxious by the time he arrives.

I see him first. A very small man with large ears that
extend out from his bald head. Never mind, I tell myself.
I do not look like a movie star either. He has small hands,
one of which he puts on my back and directs me to the
cafeteria dining room in the station. It is noisy. We have to
shout at each other. He tells me his wife died of an infection from her rheumatoid arthritis medication. She became
ill one night and died in the hospital the next day. He tells
me how much she loved music and that he has endowed
an annual concert in her name at the local high school. He
was a manager of retirement funds. He is active in his Universalist church. He is the head of many committees. I am
Jewish, I tell him. He says many Universalists are Jewish.
Were Jewish, I think but don't say. Could I ever be with a
man who sits in a pew in a church? I who once wanted to
live on a barge by the Seine and quote T. S. Eliot until the
dawn, could I live in a suburban home and go to church on
Sundays, even a church that makes less of Christ than most?
I must not slam doors, I say to myself. I need a new world,
I remind myself. He tells me that he is on a committee
that purchases art for the local university. I am impressed.
He asks me about my work, about my children. He listens
carefully. We agree to meet again. He is off to an appointment at some bank. As we part, he kisses me on the mouth.
I was just kissed by a strange man, I say to myself. It makes
me want to cry, this kiss. It's the wrong kiss, the wrong
man.

• • •

Some years ago we formed a dinner party group with four other couples. We met once a month at one of our houses and the host made a dinner, set the table with the best dishes, and we did this so that we could know each other better, become closer and closer. In a city, friends whirl about, one can go from month to month without speaking to those one holds dear and then you slip from their lives as they slip from yours. We had our dinners to hold on to each other. H. enjoyed cooking his best meals when these dinners were at our house. A week or so before the date he would take all the cookbooks and spread them out on our table and read through them, until he declared his menu. Now we are nine. I go alone. At the first dinner after H.'s death I did my best to join in conversation. The nineness of us was obvious. No one said anything, no one mentioned his name. I managed the evening well enough. I decided to cook myself for our next meeting, which was to be at our house—no, my house. I am not a cook. I haven't the patience or the skill or the interest. H. loved cooking because he said it was like chemistry, his first passion.

But I take out the cookbooks. I make a list and gather my ingredients. I cook the meal. Everyone says it is wonderful but they would say that even if I had served peanut butter and jelly sandwiches. I look around the table. My friends are here, which seems right, good. A toast to H. is proposed. I join in lifting my glass. I am glad that I can say his name in public again. Not saying his name was unnatural. He did not vanish. I remember him. I need my friends to remember him too.

Some months go by and we are having our group dinner at a nearby house. But this time my friends are talk-

ing about the various remarkable trips they are taking or
have just taken. One couple has just returned from a town
in Mexico. They walked the cobblestone streets and visited the charming churches and took a course in Spanish.
Another is off to the Caribbean to spend a week on the
white beaches of Turks and Caicos. They spoke of other
trips to Rome with their children, to Paris where the best
restaurants were named. Another couple is going to the
Arizona desert. The wife spoke of the trip she and her husband had taken a few years ago to South America where
because of her work they were greeted at the airport by
a chauffeur-driven car and treated as celebrities. There is
talk of trips taken to Sicily and weeks spent in Asia and
one man tells the story I have heard before of his journey
on a private railroad car (provided by a famous judge) to
the great Hindu sites and palaces in India. I sit silently. I
have no trips planned. Someone is going to Istanbul in the
fall. Someone else tells the story of a summer in Tuscany
twenty-five years ago. I have heard this story before. I do
not want to travel without H. I do not want to go out in
the world alone at least not yet. My lack of a traveling companion keeps me homebound, boringly homebound.

Of course we went places. Best of all we went fishing in
Alaska for fifty-pound salmon. H. would stare at the water
willing the fish to take his lure. I would admire the puf-
fins passing by. I shivered in the cold spray but the waiting
was rewarded, the waiting itself on the gray sea, with the
distant mountains, with the bear at the shoreline, with the
dive of the dolphins at the boat's side, was a memory I trea-
sured. I also have a small stone with a fossil embedded in its
center, it's of a tiny fish, clearly a fish, now stained orange.

The stone sits by my computer. I don't want to talk about my past trips. I suspect that I have washed ashore and will so remain.

This is not necessary. I could find a friend to travel with me. I could go alone. But I can't, not yet. This conversation about flights and exotic places—one couple has been to Bangladesh and another has met with the chief justice of South Africa—lasts and lasts, through the first course, into the second. I could change the subject but I don't have the will. Also I am not sure it is fair of me to shift the subject when everyone else is enjoying the conversation. I am silent, which is rare. Then as I push the food about my plate, appetite gone, it comes to me, perhaps I don't belong at this dinner anymore. Perhaps the coupled life of everyone else shuts me out in a way that I had not anticipated. This does not mean that I must lose my friends. It means that I need new friends who are not coupled, who have no trips planned. I see an advertisement on television for a cruise on a large white boat, a hotel with many stories that floats across a brilliant blue sea. I see an orchestra, waiters bearing champagne on silver trays. A couple dances in the moonlight on the deck. She wears a pink chiffon dress and a wedding ring. If there are sharks swimming in that sea they are not caught in the camera lens. Where do widows go to pass the time? If only there were a camp for us like the camps for the overweight kids advertised in the back of the *New York Times Magazine*. I could start a camp, cabins in the woods of Maine for singles over a certain age.

·   ·   ·

V. calls again. He has waited a few weeks. I almost forgot
him. He tells me he has been busy writing papers for his
courses at his local university. We agree to meet on the
next Saturday and go to the Metropolitan Museum after
lunch. This is my favorite kind of Saturday. I think about
the Universalist Church. I prefer a fiercer kind of religion
if one is going to have a religion at all. I like a thundering
Jehovah and can even understand a bleeding Christ, but a
church that is nice and understanding and modern seems
like a hospital lobby to me, an anteroom to the real story.
At lunch he tells me about his family. He grew up on a poor
farm in Nebraska. His mother had only a wood-burning
stove until he was fourteen. He worked on the farm every
day before he went to school. He went on scholarship to a
liberal arts college in California and from there to gradu-
ate school to become a professor of history but at the time
positions in academia were scarce and so he went into business instead. I think of him on the farm. This is the farm of
my childhood imagination where Indians circled and good
men and women worked with their hands to make a living
from the earth while fighting off drought and locusts and
the foreclosing bank and the storms that came each year.
In my urban mind this farm was America, a real America.
I could love a man who came from such a place, maybe.
H. came from Brooklyn and his parents were immigrants
who worked in a cigar factory and spoke Yiddish and had
escaped the czar's edicts. I understood that. I knew that
world. V.'s farm was a mystery, an alien mystery. This was
becoming interesting. He asks me if I like hiking. I do
but have not done a lot of formal walking around in the
woods, not since my camp days. V. goes on group hikes up

the mountains of New Hampshire. He has a business appointment and has to cancel our afternoon at the museum. We stand outside the restaurant where we had lunch and a cold wind blows about my ears and my nose is turning red. He kisses me and holds me close. The hug seems to be a promise of future meetings. But perhaps it is a good-bye hug. Could I love this man? I could try, I decide.

· · ·

On the other hand why should I try? Trying is not the way to loving I'm sure. Also I think that we are too different, come from such unlike worlds, that I would lose myself along the way. But if I am a real person with a memory and a history of my own I can't get lost or can I?

· · ·

Then there is K., who lives across the street. For the last years I have seen him walking up and down the street carrying groceries, wearing shorts in the coldest of weather. He is a tall man with a wide chest, three sons each well over six foot five. He has a sad beat-up Irish face. He has always looked at me kindly, offered to carry my packages, once he put an umbrella up over my head. He is never seen in a suit and a tie. He is a widower. His wife has been gone about five years. He wanders, still boyish, an old athlete, up and down. In the afternoon he goes to the park to jump rope to keep in condition. He stops me on the street. The building gossip has told him that H. has died. "How are you?" he asks. I shrug. His eyes fill with tears. "It's the loneliness," he says, "the loneliness." "You could," I say, "go to dinner with me one evening." "I could," he says. A few days later there is a message on my machine from him. "Go down, " he says, "to the park and you will see on the left of the path the snowdrops my wife Linda planted there. She brought them back from my grandmother's house and they are blooming. " It's March. I did not know that flowers bloomed in the cold winds off the drive. The next morning I go and look. There they are, white petals, shining in the thin grass, their stems thrusting up from the cold, dark ground. "I saw the flowers," I say to his machine. "They are beautiful." I thought he might call. He doesn't.

· · ·

Today there is a fog out my window. The Empire State Building has disappeared. The mist hangs over the rooftops and the water towers. I see the pipes reaching upwards, green and black on the tops of nearby brownstones. The terraces below hold summer chairs, a wilted plant or two, a rain-soaked barbeque. The traffic lights at the end of the block float and shimmer. The gargoyles on the building down the avenue are shrouded as an occasional wing or fang appears above the stone arches. Yesterday I went to Brooklyn to see my daughters and their children. I am fortunate to have their affection. I am fortunate to be welcome always in their homes. I am thankful for their company. I am also worried about this delicate matter of how much a presence I should be in their lives. How dependent on them could or should I become? In other cultures the old mother moves in with her daughter, helps with the care of the children, does the cooking. It is not unreasonable for the old to depend on the young, to be in their households as the young were once protected by their parents. And yet the idea appalls. Perhaps if I were in an Orthodox Jewish family, or an Old World Italian family, or a Navajo Indian family, I would have none of this unease but as it is I think I should be soon ready to pull away a little further, to call and be called less often, to hear fewer details of their days. I should be fading not entirely but somewhat from their view.

We gather at one daughter's house, a small rented carriage house behind a brownstone on a tree-lined street. You enter through a narrow gate and walk down a path between buildings barely wide enough for an adult to pass. The house has a small garden but now it is winter and the ground is cracked and an abandoned doll is lying in the dirt. The living-room floor is covered with the two-year-old's drum, a rag doll, a dress-up box from which tulle and taffeta burst and velvet hats and beads fall. The little girls will pull on satin dresses, bonnets, aprons, lace capes.

They will turn into princesses and mermaids. Why are they not warriors or pirates or space explorers? Diana of the hunt has been dropped from the pantheon of goddesses. What happened to the breaking of barriers that was my generation's contribution to this future? Is it over already?

There on the table waits our usual fare of bagels and whitefish and smoked salmon. H. always prepared brunch. He would have added apples and cider and quiche. The computer on a table by the couch is running a slide show of photographs of all of us, again and again. It is hard not to watch as the photos change. There for an instant I see H. with a large fish in his arms and a wide smile, sun reflecting off his dark glasses. My other daughter arrives with her three-year-old. She sits in front of the computer and checks her e-mail. Her back is toward me and the room. A cell phone rings. My stepdaughter and her husband and her ten-year-old arrive and use the chairs around the dining table for seats. The ten-year-old has been at a sleepover with a friend and now is pale and tired and bored and curls up in her father's lap. The three-year-old is hit with a drumstick by the two-year-old and screams and sobs. Her mother comforts her. Her aunt distracts her. The two-year-old is sent for a time-out. The conversation between the sisters rises and falls. So many things are left unsaid. Everyone wants to be pleased to be together. The little girls now are cutting strips of Play-Doh. They are preparing a pretend dinner. I have read too many *New Yorker* short stories, I think. I am looking through a glass darkly. The problem is with the way I am looking, not with the glass.

The sons-in-law do not dislike each other, I think. But there is an awkwardness anyway. Despite the fact that they are both lawyers they cannot think of anything to say to each other. "How did I get here, in this company?" I hear each of them silently whispering to the God of Family Life, who if not malevolent is certainly mischievous. I ask a legal question about a trial in the news. A conversation begins and winds down. Time passes slowly. I now want to go home. How is this possible?—after all, I am here with my family. If H. were here he would be clearing plates. He would be quiet too, expecting me to begin a conversation.

I do not want to be a burden to those I love: not now in my healthy years nor when I may become frail or needy. I do not want to spoil an evening of theirs, to intrude on a conversation of theirs, to steal a moment from the prime of their days. And yet now I need my daughters to call me, to anchor me, to know me. That's all right as long as I keep the balance clear. As long as I don't cross some invisible line and become like an unwanted growth on their family lives. They need their privacy, their secrets from me. I need to keep mine from them, or do I?

Do I have any secrets?

The fog has thickened. Now I can't see to the end of the street. I am hoping that someone will call me. What do I want to talk about? Perhaps the article in the *New York Times* that I read hours ago and wanted to share with H. Perhaps I want to tell someone that when I came home from Brooklyn yesterday there was a letter waiting in my mailbox from H.'s ex-wife. She is not the person who sued me whom I cannot write about. She wants me to pay her the alimony for the entire month in which H. died. The letter is addressed to the executor of his estate. She won't use my name. She wants the last drop of honey from the pot. She has in fact sued us several times over the thirty-nine years of our marriage. She hired accountants to go over our taxes, convinced that we were hiding money from her. Nothing has ever been found. Nothing had ever been hidden. She had notified the IRS at least five years running that we were cheating. Each year for five years running the IRS audited and found nothing. We weren't cheating. Now I rage. I think I won't pay her this last small amount. I think I will make her take me to small-claims court. I am spoiling for a fight. I sit at my computer and write her a letter. I tell her she is a parasite and has lived her life as a parasite. I offer to find her a social worker who can put her in touch with an organization that can aid the elderly in distress. I want to humiliate her although I realize that what might humiliate me would likely not faze her at all. Money is for her an absolute so fine that she will fight for the smallest amount, scratch out my eyes for several dollars, feel victorious when she receives it. And then again perhaps now she really needs it. I watch the mist swirl by. I feel guilty. I could find some kindness in my heart and send her the check.

Psychoanalysts (H.) always distinguish between thought and action. It is human to have wild and nasty thoughts, to wish one's enemy dead or worse. In the privacy of the mind ethics can be thrown to the wind, kindness is unnecessary, savagery permissible, blood flows freely. In the actual world of course better behavior is required, not just to avoid jail, but to soothe the conscience, and preserve decency: to be able to look at oneself in the mirror.

I decide not to send the letter. I will pay her, at least I will pay her a prorated amount based on the last fourteen days of H.'s life, the fourteen days he lived in December for which he now owes her posthumous alimony. Truth is that this cloistered, bitter, eighty-five-year-old sparrow-sized lady who has spent her life on a sparrow ledge, eating sparrow food, her twig-like legs and arms moving to protect against a danger always expected but never arrived, cannot hurt me in any significant way. It is the absence of H. that brings the unrelenting storm to my shores.

I CAN'T SEE THE MOON OUT MY WINDOW. THERE IS A FAINT golden haze up in the dark sky. It has no shape or form. It is there although I can't see it. I hear a flock of helicopters approaching. They are patrolling the city, up one side and down the other. Their lights blurred, their bug shapes indistinct, their noise coming closer, and with it some threat, invasion of terrorists, plague, fire. I sit at my window and watch the helicopters until they disappear behind the backs of the apartment buildings a few blocks away.

V. takes another month before he calls. We agree to meet for lunch when he is in town next. He calls; we arrange a lunch. On the morning of the lunch I wash my hair and put on my new red sweater. I am attempting to close the latch on my bracelet when the phone rings. He has a meeting at his church. He isn't coming into town. He says he will call me. He doesn't call. Of course he is right. We are not meant for each other. My willing suspension of disbelief was nine-tenths wish and one-tenth amazement at the situation in which I find myself.

Do I want to meet another man? I wake with the question on my divided mind. It has been three months since I told M. to go away. He would have gone eventually by himself. He was somewhat gone even when he was here. But I have met no one else. I have heard of widows who went on trips and found a new love abroad. I have heard of widows who moved into new towns and found a man while waiting to buy stamps at the post office. I know of

men and women in assisted-living arrangements who fall
in love over the bingo games or at the four o'clock movie.
I am too young and healthy for an assisted-living arrangement. Also I wonder if my desire for a new love is not a
bluff, a way of getting through without admitting to myself
that I cannot imagine a new attachment. I am pinned like a
butterfly in this sterility: drying out.

·   ·   ·

I see the Tom Stoppard play *Voyage*. I go with dear friends.
The play is about the hopeful and perhaps ridiculous politics and philosophy of young Russian men in the middle of
the nineteenth century, while Russia was still a monstrous
feudal world with most of the population held in serfdom,
a real slavery. The scenery moves, waves of water seem to
come forward and slide backwards. A man sails off and we
see him recede in depth. Beds rise from the floor, a ginger
cat who represents the death to come, the grim uncaring
mockery of human aspirations, dances across the stage. I
remember when I wanted to change the world. When we
thought that Negro men and women would be our friends
and our children raised in a world of racial equality. I remember when I thought that the winds of social change
would blow forever, bringing education and health to all.
I wanted to be a nurse in Appalachia so that I might make
sure that milk was available to small children and shoes
were worn on feet. The characters on stage end up ex-
iled, or dead of TB. The world that followed them was
worse than the world they wanted to change. I am so old
now that I am afraid of change. Something more horrible
than all that I know may wait in the shadows. Is this de-

pression? Is this realism? Is this simply the result of having lived through two-thirds of the last century? Is this why old people become conservative? You begin to fear that if you remove one rotting brick the entire edifice may fall down on your head.

Once I took buses and trains down to the Washington Mall to protest the war in Vietnam. I marched with my women friends to support a woman's right to choose. I wanted to choose another child, but that didn't matter. I thought that each of us, adding our voices, our votes, our messages on what was then an invisible screen, would bring fate to its knees, force it to do our bidding. I knew but forgot that while the Enlightenment made its mark, the worst happened anyway. The smoke of Auschwitz overcomes Goethe and Beethoven. Progress is a splinter in fate's eye. A few tears wash it out.

Of course I don't want my children to know this. I won't tell them.

H. was in the Battle of the Bulge. He didn't tell me that until we had been married thirty-five years. It slipped out in a conversation I overheard at a picnic. He didn't want to talk about the war. He had the usual affection for Franklin Delano Roosevelt of a Brooklyn boy born of immigrant parents. When it turned out that his hero had betrayed the Jews, refusing even to bomb the train tracks that would at least slow down the killing machine, he was not surprised. He was a Freudian after all and while Freud had not so much to say about politics he had everything to say about human nature and if the savage heart of man beats ever on in our breasts then the indiscriminate use of machetes lies in our future. That's what H. believed. He voted. He had opinions on the worth and substance of our political leaders. He listened to Mozart and Bach and was especially fond of sopranos. He forgave Roosevelt. But he knew what he knew. When reports came of serial killers in the Midwest, pederasts kidnapping little boys, Serbs rounding up Bosnians and the other way around and bodies in the ditches, he was not surprised. I was. I knew what he knew but I didn't want to know it.

And now that he is gone I know what he would have said about the headlines, about the editorials, about the nightly news. I know whom he would have hated and whom he would have admired. His mind follows mine about. This is what the platitude means about how the dead live on in our memory. They don't. Our memories contain knowledge of the dead, the smell of them, the sound of them, the touch that was but isn't anymore—which is good, at least if the dead one is more loved than hated. But this memory is just a memory and does not mean the dead, like a friendly ghost, like a presence that gives you the shivers, live on. H. would find such a conceit ridiculous. He would not consider my thoughts about him equivalents or adequate substitutes for his life itself. If I remember something about him, the Irish cap he wore, the time we drank ice-cold root beer at a road stand in Vermont, that is my memory sending neurons scattering about my brain. It is not his memory, which has disappeared into protein and atom, molecule and dust. Freudians do not believe in life after death, and neither do their spouses.

Which I admit deprives us of certain easy comforts. No meeting again in some heavenly place, no holding hands on a cloud, no merging of body and soul, not ever again.

I see his features, one or two in the children's faces. I see the shadows that deepened under his eyes in the shadows under a grandchild's eyes. I see his gifts repeated in their gifts. I do not see him.

I have lunch with a writer friend whose last books have all been on aging and dying and the disappearance of his self, which he finds intolerable. I understand this grieving for yourself. But I know that H. would shrug. Some people he would say cannot accept their mortality, their unimportance. The blow to their ego shatters them. Anger at the fact of death, that H. would recognize and respect. He had it too; although I can't remember his expressing it directly, I could feel it in him in the last few years of his life, a kind of darkness that would come across his face, unprovoked by any event in our lives. Anger that we must lose our bodies and our minds, which are not two things but one, is reasonable as long as it doesn't encroach too badly on the time left. My writer friend will not allow biology to run right over him without a huge complaint.

It will do him no good. Biology is unimpressed by the human capacity to describe its devastation or rant against its ways.

·   ·   ·

I am having a difficult day: an especially difficult day. I am tired. It's only noon. H. would say I am tired because I'm sad. I don't feel sad, not directly, not clearly. I feel tired behind the eyes as if I had been working for hours on a manuscript with small type. I feel tired as if I had not slept. But I had. I feel bone-tired as if I had walked five miles. I had not. I do not want to talk to a friend. I do not want to go out to lunch. I do not want to read a book or listen to music. I am a sea of negativity, a languid sea that heaves against the shore, withdraws and heaves again.

I am worried about money. But then I often worry about money without this exhaustion following. I am concerned about my daughters. Suddenly this peril or that looms large. I have no particular reason to fear for their lives but I am fearing nevertheless. A young husband could die, a desired job be denied, a piece of work be rejected, a granddaughter sicken. I am inventing disasters that have not yet happened. This is the worst waste of time imaginable. It's a tic that comes and goes and with H.'s death seems to occur more frequently. I am worried about getting sick myself and requiring nursing care, nursing home care. That is a horrible prospect. I wonder how so many people allow themselves to end up strapped to wheelchairs in dingy rooms, waiting for unkind aides to dress them. Is breath so precious that most people accept it on any terms at all?

H. and I knew a writer who in his late sixties had a small but meaningful stroke and after that he talked of the end of civilization, the coming of nuclear night, the overthrow of democracy in America, the inevitable destruction of Israel by its Arab neighbors. H. said our writer friend was confusing the end of the world with his own end. It was easier to think about the coming conflagrations of continents than of the slowly blocking arteries of his own heart. I am thinking about the rising seas due to global warming. I am thinking of the children in refugee camps in far corners of Africa. I am thinking they will die before help arrives. In my mind's eye I see a truck loaded with wheat and oranges headed for the border. I see a mine explode and the truck turn over on its side. I too am confusing my own existence with the roll of history. Also I am lonely.

How to describe this loneliness without becoming maudlin or unbearable? In the theater last night where I saw a play with two friends, a play about an English prosperous family, set in 1905, a drawing-room comedy where the tragedy broke through, I wanted to reach for H.'s hand in the dark. I did not want anyone else's hand. I did not want mints at intermission. I did not want the actors in the play to be better performers although that might have helped. I felt as if I had no hands, no place to reach. This is the loneliness that I believe will not be banished as the hours and the days and the years pass. It makes me tired, tired behind the eyes. In the children's book *Goodnight Moon*, there is a little old rabbit lady sitting in a rocking chair knitting and she is whispering "Hush" to the little rabbit who is going to sleep. Yes, I am the little old lady but I feel as if someone is whispering "Hush" to me. And I am not ready yet.

·   ·   ·

A friend calls and we talk about the Russian revolution, the evils of Stalin, the hopes of several Democratic candidates for president, the possibility that America will become a theocracy, and then we dissect a TV series we both follow with idiotic devotion, and she invites me to a dinner party in a few weeks. The sun is high and large squares and rectangles of light reflect on the walls of my living room, stripes of sunlight fall across my dining table, across the wooden chairs, over the Oriental rug H. and I bought together so

many years ago. I go for a walk. I buy a new beautiful yellow scarf. I talk to one of my granddaughters on the phone.
I am going to a movie with a friend whose husband is out
of town tonight. Ah the sweetness of it.

·   ·   ·

I have read about widowhood. The books say that after a
while the departed spouse becomes a comforting memory.
In other eras widows consulted with psychics in an attempt
to reach the beloved in a space between here and there as
if the dead were suspended between heaven and earth and
could migrate from one to another the way a monarch butterfly transverses the continent. I have always had pity for
those at the séance table. Their need is great and so is their
folly. The medium has a child appear in a cloud of light and
pretend to relay messages from the other side or doors slam
and cold air is blasted through the room or mechanically
the table rises and falls. The medium is a con artist. The
bereaved is desperate to believe. I have no desire to com-
municate with H. We had our chance. We did as well as we
could. I do not feel his presence comforting my days. I feel
his absence. There is my cold blast of air.

·   ·   ·

I have gone to the doctor. He has offered me Paxil. Paxil
will help me through. Paxil will make it easier for me to
move along. I take the Paxil. A few days into the drug I
feel calmer, steadier, better. But I stop taking it. I intend
to take it but I keep forgetting and then I decide to quit. Is
this rational or is this puritanism without a point? I am not
sure. But I know that what I was experiencing before I took

the Paxil was neither unusual nor truly unbearable. I would immediately take morphine for cancer pain. I do take Advil for headaches. I cannot count the number of times anti-biotics must have saved my life. I do have a glass of wine with dinner. I am afraid, however, that with Paxil racing through my bloodstream I will lose my edge, my observant eye will close, my wit will melt. I can reverse this decision at any moment. I am not bound by it and have signed no contract to be drug-free for the rest of my life. That said, I am off the Paxil.

.   .   .

I drop my gym membership. I just don't get there. Lazy perhaps, uninterested in my heartbeat, certainly. The rows of cycles, the televisions blinking, flashing, mouths on multiple screens opening with words only for those with attachments in their ears, wires plugged into machines, a curious silence in the long rectangular room, do not warm me, not right now. The rows of lockers, the women in vari-ous stages of undress, the towels thrown in a bin, it is not like a walk in the park, or a swim in the ocean, or meeting a friend for lunch. I avoid the mirrors in the gym. Ultimately I avoid the gym.

.   .   .

We have our first Seder without H. We have it at the Brook-lyn home of my daughter, whose husband will lead. In other years H. sat at the head of the table and directed the reading of the Haggadah, using his deepest, most serious voice. He also cooked the food, poured the soup and carved the meat and filled the plates with vegetables. He was proud of his recipes. He told us how his father would make wine in their cellar in Brooklyn for the Seder each year. This was only until the family was evicted during the Depression from their home, a fact which H. did not say aloud, because he wished to forget, because he was ashamed, because he had traveled to a different America even if his daughters were back in Brooklyn now. My son-in-law has invited two colleagues from his office. The furniture in their small living room has been pushed aside and the couch is sitting on their terrace. The tablecloth is ice-white. Wedding presents are used for the first time, bowls and spoons and candlesticks display themselves proudly. Crystal glasses catch the light and shine. Everyone has arrived, everyone who is coming that is. My stepdaughter and her husband and three children, my other daughter with her husband and her child, and me.

We begin to tell the story of the exodus from Egypt and the parting of the Red Sea and the flight from slavery toward the promised land and we read what this rabbi or that had to say about this detail or that. The little girls get up from the table and the ten-year-old plays with them. We ignore the distraction. But I am distracted. My face is serene. But I have become hollow, as if I am not there at all but a pretender sits in my place. I think nothing. I refuse to think about H.'s absence. I have taken flight. This is the trick of bored schoolchildren, airline passengers waiting out a storm, people in doctors' offices, on subway trains. I turn the pages at the right moment. I read aloud what I am asked to read but I hear nothing.

The mournful rhythm of the Hebrew words, Eliahu Rachamim, Elijah the Merciful, float up around me. A little child goes to the door to open it for Elijah and everyone sings the prayer as the invisible visitor joins our table, takes a sip of the wine set aside in a large goblet just for him, leaves again. The child closes the door and returns to the table. In other years I have felt a shiver of awe as the door opens, a lump in my throat as I pledge myself to the generations that have gone before, opening and closing the door, and I am aware that those in line to the crematorium sang this song, and I know that all over in other homes at almost the same moment, Elijah enters and retreats. Of course Elijah's visits are merely metaphors of rescue. His magic way of being everywhere at once is no more than a plea for comfort in a non-comforting universe. This year I am not appeased. Santa Claus, the Easter bunny, the tooth fairy, Elijah, it's all the same, a fairy tale to enchant the children, to allow the adults to return to their childhood when anything was possible. In other years I have listened with great care, thought about the wise son and the wicked son, and I have sung the songs with full voice, the same songs we sing each year, the songs of praise, of hope. This year someone who seems to be me mouths the words along with the others, helps clear the table, places the dishes in the dishwasher, watches the small children climb into their mothers' laps, tired now, enough of it all.

But then in the light of the candles now burned down halfway I see the flush of my daughters' faces, wine of course but also the relief of having served the meal with all its dishes, with having said the words once more. I see the Haggadahs on the table covered now with crumbs and several with wine stains. The matzoh balls were soft, the brisket was sweet, a cat in the garden below calls out for a mate. I see my sons-in-law, large men, different one from another. I see my smallest granddaughter holding her doll in her arms and pressing matzoh into her never opening mouth. The room is warm and crowded. My stepdaughter is explaining why she hated a recently seen movie to her half-sister, who loved the movie. They both raise their voices. This is a friendly discussion and a not-so-friendly discussion. I join them. I divert them.

There had to be a first Seder that H. couldn't make. This is not a surprise. Someone had to take over his place at the head of the table.

A few blocks away the lights on the Brooklyn Bridge blur in the soft rain that is beginning to fall. There are no stars out that we can see from the small terrace but that doesn't mean they aren't there, gas and rock, meteor and planet. Soon bunches of lilacs will rise on their long branches out of black plastic buckets at the greengrocers'.

Later on the way home I return to myself. I am half-asleep and at peace. Maybe the wine finally had its effect, the sweet wine that no one likes but me, that I could drink by the bucketful. It was a beautiful Seder, a promising Seder, one that will go on without me one day, and that is how it should be. Between my thumb and forefinger I rub the pearls that I am wearing. These are the pearls that H. had given me. Actually I gave one of the double strands to my stepdaughter when she was married. H. replaced it, not without complaint and he made me wait about ten years and my strands don't match. These are not magic pearls. They do not summon up H. from the depths of the underworld. One day I will give them to a granddaughter but not yet.

. . .

One death reminds you of others. Rather one death like a
magnet picks up other deaths, making a pile. I don't think
too often about my mother's death. She was fifty-two and
I was twenty-seven. She died of a melanoma that began
with a neglected mole and ended with a brain tumor. This
was in the days when chemotherapy was almost unknown.
Six months later my father would marry his mistress with
whom he had a twelve-year-old child. I would be divorced
from my husband within two months. My mother lost her
life before she had a chance to brave the world and produce
a play. She wanted to be a producer. My mother died before she had a chance to run a business. She had a head for
the stock market and she remembered every card played
and was unbeatable at canasta and gin and backgammon.
She died before she understood that she didn't have to be
neglected, rejected, and weepy every night. As I watched
her die I was in shock. I had not before believed that such
a thing could happen, happen to someone I knew so well,
could shake the ground on which I stood. It could be argued
I stood too close to her. It could be said that we talked on
the phone too often. It could be said that I had not learned
to stand on my own two feet. It could be said that although
I rejected the life she had wanted me to lead—a lady of
much leisure, married well to a man of a certain position
and a membership in a golf club—I was still my mother's
child. Every day for two months I visited her bedside, with
my young daughter from what would soon be my first marriage playing with a jewelry box on the carpet below. I saw
the gray hair on her head begin to grow, an inch and inch

and a half, as if death itself were pushing forward, insisting on its rights. She soon lost her speech and I could see the terror in her eyes. My father ordered a speech therapist to teach her to speak, to learn the letters of the alphabet again. This was done so that she wouldn't know she was dying. But she was not fooled. I could see it in the way she turned her head away from the therapist, the way she used her good hand to sweep off the bed the crayons and the paper the lady had brought.

I missed the exact moment that she died but came a half hour later. I could see that life had gone, that her skin was a different texture, that her eyes were sinking back into her head and that she seemed to be a bluish color and her bright red nails—the manicurist had come the day before—seemed too bright, too loud, for the body that was shrinking into itself right there before my eyes.

It took me months to understand that the tragedy was her life and not her death, which had been without pain and had not caused years of suffering. It took me months to understand that there was nothing unusual in her dying. Yes, it was too soon, she was still young enough to have enjoyed so many things, but the cemetery where we buried her, on a hill overlooking the swift-moving Hudson River, was dotted everywhere with stones. My experience could not be unique. I put a stone on her grave. I grew up.

But now with H.'s death I find I am thinking about her again. Her cigarette in her hand, her eye makeup running down her cheeks, her mystery novels on her bed, the crossword puzzles she could do in moments, the way she smelled of powder and sweat and scented soap and her eyes would swell and the skin beneath them puff up when she wept, which she often did. I remember the bowl of ice by her bedside which she used with cotton wads to reduce the swelling. I remember waiting in the lobby while she had her hour with her psychoanalyst. He tried to rescue her I'm sure. He didn't succeed. Now suddenly I think of her. She has been dead so long now. She never knew H. or the two children we had together. She would have loved my step-daughter and taken her to tea at the Plaza and to Saks Fifth Avenue on shopping trips. She would have been surprised by how the story followed on after her death. Now once in a while I think of her at night. I try to think only kind thoughts. I am the only one alive to think of her.

.   .   .   .

Of course one's children don't live happily ever after although I admit I had some expectations that they might. I take from the table in the living room a large photo in a silver frame of one of my daughters in a wedding dress kissing a handsome groom and consider what to do with it now. I could put it in a bureau under a pile of old sweaters. I could put it in a drawer. I could wrap it in a bag from the market and leave it out the back door where it will disappear with the remains of dinner. I am not sure. I had loved the photo or the illusion that the photo gave of time frozen, white silk rustling, fortune looking kindly down. Divorce is not such an uncommon outcome, leaving me with two sons-in-law where once I had three. I had even considered it on the day the photo was taken. An Uninvited Wedding Guest. I saw Him in the corners of the dance floor. I saw Him standing stiffly at the end of the receiving line as I shook hand after hand.

Divorce has lost its capacity to surprise or scandalize. It still scalds. I put the picture in a closet on a high shelf. This is not a tragedy. I don't have an exact name for what it is. Perhaps it is simply a short paragraph in the book of family life. I fight off a desire to put down the book.

.   .   .

Touch. I took it for granted. H. took my arm when we were walking in the street. He took my hand in the movies. He lay his head in my lap while reading the Sunday paper. He rubbed my shoulders when I was stiff. He wrapped his legs around mine while he slept. In the shower we soaped one another. In the kitchen we leaned into each other. And then, not as often as we did a decade ago, we did all those things that although most private are usual among human adults. We lay afterwards body to body, my head on his chest, his arms around me, breathing softly together: even the night before he died.

And now I think I may never know another man so well. I may never again even hold hands in a movie or feel an arm across my back. Many women live this way, old and young too: untouched. We know that babies if they are not held in human arms do not thrive. They do not smile or turn over, or stand. H. worked with babies whose mothers were too sad or dismayed by their own lives to hold their children. H. worked to help the mothers look into the eyes of their children. H. taught me that the human infant must be rocked and touched and wiped and soothed by another's smell, flesh against flesh. I think perhaps at the other end of life this might be true also. Or else one dies quickly.

This, judging by the millions of elderly who do not

die, at least not immediately, and not from lack of partners, cannot be true. But is it true for me?

I am constantly losing my keys, my glasses, my watch. I spend too much time each day looking for lost papers, for a pen, for a stamp, for a sock. It's as if the physical world of ordinary objects is playing with me, maliciously teasing me. More likely I am playing with the physical world, using it to prove that I have indeed lost something, something that will not be found in the hamper or under the newspaper or behind the bookcase.

I am going to meet a friend at the theater. I am about halfway down the subway stairs when I hear my name. Someone is calling me. I turn around. I look up. K. in his T-shirt and shorts is standing above leaning over the railing. "Are you free for dinner tomorrow night?" he shouts down. "Yes," I answer. "Come at seven," he adds and disappears. Unreasonably, I am pleased.

The next night I arrive at his door with a bottle of wine taken from one of the cases H. had bought that still rest at the back of my hall closet. K. is making dinner. His apartment is furnished in frat-boy style, dark, spare, no rugs, no curtains, no flowers. No woman since before the flood. We talk. I find out many things about him. He went to an Ivy League college. He played football in high school. He went to law school and became, in a desultory sort of way, a lawyer for musicians. He has no practice now. He jumps rope in the park to stay thin. He is learning to play the flute. His three grown sons are fighting over his wife's legacy. He had divorced his wife several years before her death because, as he said, they "set to squabbling." His dad had owned an auto repair shop in upstate New York. He had not married until he was nearly forty. He has watery blue eyes. He has the gentle way of large men. I am happy in his company. "Perhaps we can go to a movie together one night," I suggest. "I could do that," he answers. But then he never calls. When I see him on the street I smile and wave but do not stop.

There is no point in imagining what was so hard about calling me to go to a movie. I know it was not his dislike of me. I give up thinking about it. But what stays in my head is his story, the unfathomable parts as well as the others. I think about his two sons. I hold his life in my mind. Then I don't.

. . .

I have noticed that I am becoming irritated all too often by friends I have known and loved for years. One says something very rude about my daughter and I say nothing but my heart grows cold toward her. I have bought theater tickets with another friend and on the appointed day she says she wants to meet me at the theater and then wants to go home to fix supper for her husband. She has allowed no time to visit with me. Is she afraid that what I have is catching? Or does she just not want to be with me, or is she thinking of the check at the café we might have gone to? I don't know, but I begin to see her as an indistinct figure on a distant shore. I am irritated by another friend's tales of her childhood woes. She repeats them again and again. I have heard them thousands of times. I feel impatient when she begins. I am angry at someone's anti-Zionism. I am angry at another friend's patronizing advice that I should buy new clothes. I should but I don't want to. I am turning into a nurser of minor grievances, a person I have never been before. I may be observing the signals of the tsunami of anger that lurks within. I am envious of others, which is foolish. I am all too easily offended or bored.

I will try to be angry at what I am truly angry about and leave my friendships in calm waters.

LOOKING EAST I SEE THE MOON. IT IS A SMALL SLIVER UP in the sky. There are a few stars visible above the buildings and there is a red light blinking on a high rooftop, a warning light to low-flying airplanes. I stare into the windows across the way. I see the blue light of the televisions. I see a fern pressing against a pane. I see a silhouette moving across the window. A light turns out. I can't see in anymore. Everyone for blocks around is asleep or lying awake in the dark.

I have lost some friendships over the years. Now I regret it. I have been too quick to anger and have pulled away when staying would have been a far better thing to do. Unlike my father I do not yell loud enough to frighten the banshees in the woods. I do not directly confront, or create scenes. When I am angry I pull away and like some ancient turtle take my head inside my shell where it cannot be seen or trampled. In fact I have a terrible if silent temper. Losing friends is natural enough. We change and our interests change and we admire less a person we admired most a while ago. It is easier to be friends with those who share our occupations, our politics, our neighborhoods, our mutual friends. It is hard to hold on to friendships when people move away to another state or to another world. I am a good friend but not constant. I can be frightened away easily. I have a bad track record of holding on. I regret this.

Among my condolence notes is one from a woman I had once considered dear: Y.

Another woman, a famous writer, a brilliant writer, a right-wing writer, a passionate woman, L., who reviled me, loathed me, loathed my bones, because of my views on peace in the Middle East had told Y. not to talk to me at a public meeting. Y. obeyed. She avoided my eyes at the lunch break. She walked away from me as I approached her. Y. would not be seen walking out the door with me. I felt betrayed. It was a playground thing, it happened over a decade ago. I was a lesser writer than the writer in whose good graces she wanted to stay. Y. and I, who once had lunch often, spoke on the phone constantly, discussed people and politics, in and out, stopped speaking. We lived a block away from each other. I missed her company. Now I held her condolence note in my hand and a warm flush came over me. I called. We arranged to meet at a local café. Y. had recently lost her father, who had been in his late nineties. Y. and her father had lived in the same building. Her father had escaped Warsaw shortly after Y. herself had escaped to England. The father and daughter had remained clasped to each other into the old age of both. There was about them both an air of tragedy past, of hard times endured, of a fear of the world, a dislike of the color red, the sound of jazz or rock, or glasses tinkling in the evening. They were gray people. Lust had been left behind or so it seemed. Now she seemed pear-shaped, nun-like, long gray hair, no artifice at all, like a woman who had never known love, but she had, if only of the not-very-long-lived sort.

We talk, Y. and I, about children and grandchildren, about her father, about her work. She has a collection of stories about to be published. As I leave her an hour or so later I am lighter of heart. My friend has returned to me. I call and make a date for lunch. On the appointed day I call. She is surprised to hear from me. "Oh no, I couldn't," she says. "I ate some strawberries and broke out in hives yesterday." I had heard that before, years before. It was something she told me when she broke a date a long time ago. Then I had believed it. "Oh, well," I said, "call when you are better." Weeks went by. I am eating dinner with my stepdaughter and children in a local Mexican restaurant. I see Y. passing by. She looks in the window and sees me. I start to wave. She rushes off, turning her face away. I am in a discount clothing store on Broadway and I see her several racks away. She sees me. She rushes behind a screen and I see her furtively making her way toward the revolving door. She has pulled her scarf up over her face.

I called her again and we made a time to meet at a neighborhood place. "Did you not want to see me?" I asked, and then, as the café lattes arrived at the table, she told me: "I have a friend already, one good friend. I like my television and my apartment and I feel safe there. I do not need more friends. I would be willing to see you once a year or perhaps twice, but that's all." She is frank and

abrupt. I had always admired this in her. She has no time
for the usual formal bows or the common gestures in the
dance of public flirtation. But she is telling me to go away.

But I don't let it go. She is an odd person. I, in my
depleted world, am now less. I had hoped for a return of
our old friendship. Am I innocent in this matter? I remember that H. and I invited Y. five or six years running to
our family Thanksgivings. Her children were then away
at colleges in other parts of the country. My children were
still at home. We also had a few friends at the table. H.
cooked a huge turkey. Before the meal each person read a
poem of his or her own choosing, including the smallest
of children. Then one year as we were clearing the dishes,
Y. said to me that she thought I was using Thanksgiving
as a way of showing off my family, to pose my family,
in front of those who had less. She thought she had been
invited to be an audience to a scene of assumed family
happiness and success. Were those my motives? Not in my
conscious mind, but how could I have been so thought-
less as to imagine that she would want to share in our
Thanksgiving when she had no husband and her children
were away? Was there some element of gloating in this
Thanksgiving invitation? In fact there may have been a
competitive undercurrent to the friendship all along. We
are both writers. She more amazing than I, but I too have
published. Was envy in the mix of the friendship? Was I
reaping what I had sowed?

On Broadway I see her. She is walking toward me. A
heavy woman with wide hips, she is wrapped in a black
shawl and carrying a big bag. There is a small dowager's
hump on her back. Her shoes are sensible, heavy. She

doesn't see me at first. And then she does and she turns around and walks in the other direction. At the corner she moves quickly across to the other side of Broadway; her steps are hurried. She doesn't wait for the light to change. Perhaps a car will hit her or an approaching bus.

What I do know is that I have my own raw and jagged edges. This is a short story of friendship on the rocks.

· · ·

H. and I had an old friend, or almost friend, N. He has died in Missouri. He was determined to be a famous artist, a great writer. Unfortunately determination has nothing to do with the matter. He knocked on the door for years and finally became a writing teacher whose students loved him, because he was wild and passionate about words on the page, and because he was funny, Jewish-comic funny, and because his religion was literature. In this he was a very pious man.

He played the flute medium-well. He played poker with us, and would have won more often if he wasn't continually telling stories about famous writers he knew or reporting on conversations with ever-shifting agents and editors. Many things had happened to him in the last few years. He had heart trouble and prostate cancer and he walked with a cane and his voice was soft and blurred due to a stroke, but bravely he went on, out to dinner, to readings which he gave and parties where he sat in a corner and people leaned over to hear his words. His wife loved him. His grand-daughter loved him. His students too.

He died after a heart operation in a Missouri hospital where he had contracted not one infection but three.

I go to my shelves and pick up his novels. The books are there but unread by most of the public. They have serious themes that were common in our mutual youths, art as the only meaning in life, alienation as common as pollen in the air and sex as distraction from death. The obscurity of his novels is unimportant. The work of the writer is to write and most of us will be forgotten faster than you can say "eternity" and stamp your foot three times.

Many friends will mourn him. I see more death coming toward me. H. was not the last to die on this earth, in my world, among my friends and my family. My entire cohort will march in a line right off the cliff: a parade of souls going, going, gone. This does not come as a surprise. However, in this instance misery does not love company. I would have preferred it if H.'s death could have spared N. and all the others.

· · ·

I have gone online to Match.com. I have answered their questions truthfully. I have sent in a photo or rather I had a daughter send in a photo because the technology is a little beyond me. I wait for a response.

Two hours later I have several responses.

· · ·

I am dreaming now and in each of my dreams H. appears. He is holding the spaniel that we had before the children went off to college. The spaniel went blind in his old age and the children had lost interest in him years before. The dog's eyes were always filled with mucus, which I wiped with tissue again and again. I walked him three times a day. In my dream H. is smiling at me, or is it the dog that is smiling? Sometimes when I am awake I think of H. standing by the stove, sitting in his football-watching chair, pulling on his raincoat, searching the closet floor for his warm gloves. Last night we were together walking the streets of a city, maybe London. We are late for something. We are lost. Then H. turns down a side street and disappears. I don't see him. I wake. I sit up suddenly. The cat jumps up. He was sleeping on my chest. My dreams are not nightmares, but they are not comforting either. I am always trying to get somewhere I cannot get, or open something I cannot open. I always knew that you couldn't dream of the actual future or find portents of the days to come in last night's sleep. But I didn't know that you can't change reality, not in an orderly meaningful way, in your sleep. That is a disappointment.

When I was a small child I was shy. I remember adults telling me to speak up. I remember the dread of a first day at school, a birthday party. But then the shyness passed. I managed in strange places with new people but now with H.'s death the shyness has returned. I am going to a party where I know a few of the guests but have barely met the hosts. There will be no challenges there. No one is going to say to me, who are you and what do you think you are doing here. No one is going to turn their back on me if I approach them. But an hour before I am to leave for the party I think perhaps I won't go. It seems too much to enter a room with many people I have never seen before talking to each other. Why would anyone there want to open their circle to me? I could stay home and daydream. I could stay home and read. I could feel safe in my bed with my cat at my side. I could avoid the cold winter's night.

But I know that only a coward would stay indoors. I know that hours spent in the company of others are usually good hours. I like parties. I like to talk to people. I cannot listen to the bashful voice within me that trembles a little as I pick out something to wear for the evening, put on my coat and scarf, and check for my keys and leave my house.

At the party I talk to strangers. I introduce myself and join the conversation. I am happy. I listen and I talk. Everyone is willing to talk to me. It is a room of sociologists and law professors. It is a room of politics and feminism and old flirtations. The guests have stories, divorces, children who broke their hearts, love affairs that ended in disaster, books that were mocked, academic rewards denied, illnesses borne bravely. I don't hear those stories but they run through the party like ribbons wrapping everyone in a gentle companionship.

· · ·

I am on my way to meet a friend near Columbia University for lunch. I walk past St. Luke's emergency room. I pause. It is noon. The last time I was there it was nearly midnight. H.'s body had been placed on a steel table. His jacket and shirt had been cut off his body. His glasses were by his feet. His face was sunken and shrunk. I kissed him on the lips. I knew from the feel of his lips that he was not there. The emergency room was almost deserted. The too-bright lights cast almost no shadows. The doctors—were there two or three?—hovered about. It comes back to me now, a kind of flashback, an unwelcome intruder. I stand outside the doors and seem unable to move. I move.

· · ·

One of the responses I receive on Match.com is from a fifty-six-year-old man. I e-mail him back. I say, "I am too old for you. But you seem terrific, you will be perfect for someone." He e-mails me, "I like older women. My last girlfriend was seventy-four." I consider this. I have a peculiar prefeminist reaction. There is something unholy about a man who wants a woman almost his mother's age. It crosses some invisible boundary. Is he looking for a Simone Signoret? I do not reek of powder and smoke and perfume. I am not so worldly or wise. I do not seduce young men. Yes, an older man, a man who is protective of me, wiser in ways than me, bossy even, appeals. I recognize that I am out of date. My daughters do not care about the age of their men: way older, way younger, it has never mattered to them. But I am embedded in old-fashioned images. Fred Astaire was not a little boy to Ginger's mommy. In the movie screen of my mind I do not see them leaping across my brain only to pause as Ginger ties Fred's shoes. Humphrey Bogart was not Ingrid Bergman's son. Audrey Hepburn was never older than anyone. I e-mail back. I repeat, I am too old for you. Then comes another e-mail, a handsome forty-five-year-old, an investment banker, with a house in the south of France and one in Delray Beach, Florida. I sigh. I am too old for him too, and even if that weren't so, we are not from the same planet. It's not just that he golfs and I don't. He wants an older woman. He says so. I e-mail him back: thank you, but this wouldn't work. He takes my word for it. A chicken can fall in love with a goat I'm sure. The lines are not so firm and there are no rules in romance but I am a product of my times. I don't want to dominate and I don't want to pretend I am something I am not.

In my mail I find another letter from my husband's ex-wife. She has written it on her typewriter; the ribbon has faded so I can hardly read her missive. There are now no typewriter ribbons in the stores. Perhaps she could have found one on eBay. She sends back my check for half a month alimony and insists that because she was to be paid at the beginning of the month she is entitled to the full amount H. owed her for all of December. She wants it all despite the fact that he was not here to earn it. First I name-call, "Virago, witch, leech." Then I notice I am more amused than angry. There is a nerviness in this; one almost has to respect the persistence, bow before the madness. I see a mind oblivious to all but its self. Next she will drag me into small-claims court. An adventure I suppose. I will not pay. If it is grieving widow against hostile divorcée, I think I win. But this is shooting fish in a barrel. Has she turned me petty? Am I small-minded or justified in resistance to this claim, a last claim after a long life of parasitical subsistence? It is amazing how many occasions arise in which decisions need to be made that call ethics into play. I hear this minor theme again and again as conscience knocks against will, even in so small a matter as half the alimony check.

I am my brother's keeper. But am I my dead husband's ex-wife's keeper? That is the question.

· · ·

I go to lunch with a man who has contacted me through Match.com. He lives on the Upper West Side as I do. He reads the same magazines as I do. He once lived in the same apartment building that I grew up in. His wife has died.

His photo is slightly blurred but he doesn't look like an ax murderer. He was a science teacher and then went into his wife's family business. His children went to the school some of my grandchildren now attend. He grew up in Brooklyn very near where H. lived.

When I arrive at the café where we have agreed to meet he is standing waiting for me. I see on his face a look of deep anxiety. Is he afraid I am an ax murderer? He is a small man and looks like Woody Allen with a bad cold. God knows what I look like to him. H. was in love as a teenager with Ingrid Bergman. He didn't seem disappointed in me. The man I will call A. explains to me that he does not like to eat in public restaurants because of the potential germs and unclean kitchen conditions. He explains that he needs to wash his hands three times and his dishes three times each. He rhythmically turns his head from side to side as he speaks. Perhaps this is a tic of sorts or is he taking a quick glance at his side looking for someone wielding a knife? His fingers drum on the tabletop. His foot jiggles. I talk about myself. I ask him questions about his children and his wife. She died of lung cancer shortly after the family business was sold. They had planned many trips they never were able to take. He describes releasing her ashes in the Metropolitan Museum's Egyptian wing, which had been one of his wife's favorite places. He had slipped a packet of ashes into a small bag he strapped beneath his suit sleeve. When no one was looking he and his sons let the ashes out into the air. In the Egyptian wing there can be no other thoughts but thoughts of death and time and the human wish for eternal life. His intention was to honor his wife. However, I am now convinced that I need not visit the Egyptian wing of the Met ever again.

He tells me about his sons who are perfect and imperfect as all our children are. One has been strange all his life, brilliant but strange. The other suffers from dyslexia but seems to have a normal life, but I have not heard the whole story, not yet. Of course I cannot tell him the real long tale of my children's lives. It would take forever. He couldn't listen that long. He doesn't need the information. I couldn't begin to convey who they are, why they are who they are, in the time it takes to drink a cup of tea. All I can do is let him know that there are stories that will be told in time. I can let him know that my children consume me and have since they were born. This is true for him also. I hear it in his voice. I hear it in the way he shies away from telling me the very most important of their secrets. We are two strangers at a table in a public place. How much easier it would be if we were dogs and could smell the truth about each other and then go run in the park back and forth, jumping and tumbling in the dirt.

He remarks again and again that I speak so fluently, so well. I am a writer after all. Everyone I know speaks in long full sentences that loop and dip and soar. This man knows many things I do not. He knows about fossils and has traveled to find them on distant shores. He knows about electricity and computers and objects foreign to me. He understands calculus. His mind is very good. I am liking him more and more. Then he tells me about his childhood home. He grew up poor, very poor he says, the youngest of six boys, and in the house there was violence, the police were called again and again. He shakes his head from side to side while telling me this. Gray waves of poverty and trouble and pain flow over us. His brothers left the house and he was the one who returned from a year in Israel, and cared for his diabetic blind mother in her final years. He mutters something about sexual abuse. Did I hear that correctly? Can I ask him to repeat it? I decide to let it go. Henry Roth knows this landscape. A. has had two serious relationships since his wife died. Both of these women had personalities that were too strong, too demanding and in the end he did not like them.

Suddenly I am tired. I want to go home. I have had enough. I feel his anger under the words. I feel the anger that accompanies those who wash their hands three times to ward off evil, possibly their own evil. I cannot do this. Am I wrong? Am I aborting a romantic possibility for the wrong reasons? Am I superficial in not liking the tension in his face, the twitching, the tightness of his smile? Am I just afraid of a new person? This is very possible. Perhaps I do not intend ever to find a new companion. I will not see A. again.

When I was last in Jerusalem working on a book, before H. died, I stayed at the Inbal Hotel where many Orthodox young men and women held their first dates in the café on the main floor. In the early evening I saw them, girls as young as sixteen or perhaps a little older, boys who wore black hats and as much beard as their age allowed, white-skinned, leaning over the small tables, trying to do just what I had been doing, who are you, should you live with me for the rest of my life? It was a lovely scene, rife with hormones and the scent of marriage vows in the air, and as I watched from my table I could tell which dates were

going well and which were not. I saw the girls smile and
beckon with their eyes. I saw the boys wave their hands in
the air as they spoke. I drank in great swallows of shyness,
male and female, also great swallows of hope.

The waiters came and brought the green tea and the
lights outside the windows gleamed and the polished wood
tables served as perfect platforms to launch a new life.

But I can't do this now. Not with A. with whom one
would spend ever after, no matter that it's a short ever
after, dodging around the damage in his mind, skirting the
danger of his anger, avoiding his disapproval, wiping and
cleaning every surface so he wouldn't be affronted. Besides
there is even at my age, even after everything, a question of
desire. I thought this would not matter anymore. I thought
that companionship would suffice for my remaining days
and I would be lucky to find that but there is the stubborn-
ness of body and the peculiarity of desire. I will not be able
to ignore it.

A. calls the next day. I sound friendly. I tell him I can't
talk. Perhaps tomorrow, I say. He hears me. And he doesn't
call again. Of course that's my story. His might be that
he found me not to his taste, not to his style, not what he
wanted at all. I don't mind if that's what he thought. It
is a blessing of old age not to care if someone should not
choose to dance. I find to my delight that I have outgrown,
or perhaps outlasted, the need for every eye to shine on me
kindly.

I am asked to a luncheon and talk at the Jewish Theo-
logical Library, to view the rare book collection there.
I go. There are only five of us around a table. This is a
fund-raising effort on the part of the library. I am invited

in hopes I will be helpful in nonfinancial ways. At least I assume so, or the fund-raisers have stumbled while assembling their targets. In the 1920s the seminary library had endured a fire. Fortunately the fire had been in a different tower from where the rare treasures had been stored. The librarian sits on one side of a table pulling boxes that look like books off a cart that sits by his elbow. He opens a box with frayed and jagged pieces of parchment on it. It is a prayer book from the sixth century. The scribe had written in such careful letters and such straight lines that it almost seemed printed. The pages came from the storehouse of old papers from the Cairo synagogue. Jews do not destroy holy papers. They bury them, and these among other relics had been found in the basement of the synagogue and retrieved before the Second World War. Of course I wanted to touch the pages, but you can't. The smudge of fingers, the oil on the skin would damage the parchment. We are shown a wedding contract from the fifth century with words that translate into the same words that are on my daughters' marriage contracts. We look at a small book that is illustrated with miniature figures and tells the story of Joseph in Egypt.

Again and again appeals are made to God to hear, to forgive, to bless. Again and again praise is offered to God from the pages, pages labored over long before the printing press came into existence. Meanwhile in the communities from which these pages come, plague arrived, oppression in the form of Muslim kings or officiates of the power of the government appeared. Again and again the praise to God occurs after storms and shipwrecks and military disasters, disease cuts off the life of young children and parents

mourn their children and children mourn their parents and
the seasons change and the years pass and the monarchs
change but the prayers do not. Are they heard? Are they
ever heard?

The prayers we said at H.'s grave I wrapped around
myself to keep away the cold. But God: I tried but could
not believe that God was there with me, with my children,
on that hilltop, at that moment. H. believed in evolution,
in random accident. I believe in evolution and random
accident but I am not so sure that behind all that, the eons
and the millennia, and the Tyrannosaurus Rex, there isn't
some reason, some mind, some deity that began it all. Perhaps a cruel deity but a deity nevertheless. On the other
hand when it comes to the God within, the voice of God
that speaks in the wilderness, the one that hands Moses
a good book on a mountaintop, that infuses Buddha or
inspires Gandhi or walks on water or resurrects the dead, I
am without the ability to see. My eyes are empty sockets.

I am not a scientist but I count myself a follower of that
camp. I like harmony but am too attached to my jagged
edges to merge with any God within or God without.
Those who can have my full respect. Those who can't are
more likely to join me for a movie and a Chinese dinner
afterwards. Yoga class results in stretched muscles. Those
muscles just don't stretch all the way to eternity.

So I will not take solace in God's plan, God's love,
God's good intentions. This is ungrateful of me. Creation
no matter how long it took is good, just not quite good
enough.

Which does not mean I do not value each and every
scrap of parchment, each old Bible, each work of early

printing press and ancient scribe. Artifacts, remnants of dearly beloved convictions, messages in bottles cast upon an eternal sea, they deserve respect. They evoke awe.

A SEVENTY-FIVE-YEAR-OLD WIDOWER CONTACTS ME ON Match.com. He has a kind face. He lives in Brooklyn. He says he is looking for a companion, a friend. I e-mail him. He e-mails me again. I give him my phone number. He calls. He has a gentle manner and a soft voice. I agree to meet him on Sunday at the Botanical Gardens in Brooklyn. He is waiting at the gate when I arrive. We walk together through the paths that wind around the giant tulips, luscious reds and purples. We talk of our children and he tells me he owns a condo in Cancún and a cottage in the Adirondacks. First he worked as a longshoreman in the Brooklyn Navy Yard, then he managed his wife's family business for years. He was a pilot in World War Two. He takes my hand in his. "This is the first time," he tells me, "since my wife died, that I have held a woman's hand." He purchases sandwiches and bottles of water and we sit on the grass on a hill above some children playing ball. Then he says, "I have to tell you I am not the age I entered on Match.com." I am not surprised. A few years do not matter to me. He says, "I couldn't enter the year of birth, because the program didn't go back that far." Now I am alert. "When were you born?" I ask. "Nineteen-eighteen," he says. I do the math. He is eighty-nine. He is straight-backed, still handsome. His mind is there, his heart, the feeling heart, seems strong. But when he invites me back to his apartment in Brooklyn I make an excuse. When I get home I e-mail him that I am unable to bear another loss. He e-mails me back, "Seize the moment, let's take advantage of what time we have." He has a point. But I don't want to. I am a coward. I am unkind. He tries a few more times. He finally e-mails me, "I must accept your decision." He must. Important question: Do I, without ever quite admitting it to myself, require a man who has achieved in the world as H. did? Do I require diplomas and published papers as a prerequisite for my hand? If so, I am ashamed. On the other hand ambition and knowledge are part of who and what a person is or has become. Could I love a truck driver or a shoe salesman? Is it more sensible to be alone than to slide down the social scale? The answer to that last question is of course not. But can I do it? "Class" is such a loaded word, a Marxist word, a thing no decent American wants to talk about. But is it real, real like age, real like your Social Security number? Is class my shadow that I can't dodge no matter how I turn?

I go to dinner at my friends' home. The man is a painter, the woman a journalist. Two other couples, old friends, are there. I am happy to be with them. I have a glass of wine. The artist's paintings are on the wall, rivers of blue and green, leaf-like, water-like, fall-like, they float above us. I talk about Iran and our president and about the Picassos at the Guggenheim show of Spanish paintings. I ask about this one's biography in progress of Rosa Luxembourg, that one's article on art critics of the fifties. I ask the doctor at the table about hospice care and the right to die, and as I sit, with food on my plate, conversation, a bright slice of lemon in my water glass, a strange cloud comes over me. It is not the absence of H. I suddenly believe I am damaged and have been hiding the damage. As if I were wearing a wig, covering up the fact that I had blown off the top of my head with a handgun. It could be the drink. I am not a good drinker. These friends I have known a long time and each of them I love for different reasons. I know them so well that their stories are imprinted in my brain. I could tell them myself as it is with old friends. I am safe here in this room. If it weren't for this hole in my skull I would even be content.

· · ·

I used to read all the time. I spent a childhood in books. Now I read slowly. No, I still read quickly, but I put the book down after a few pages. I can't concentrate. I resist being pulled inside the words on the page. I seem to think it too dangerous to embrace the words on the page. This is odd. My old escape, my familiar room in my brain, is no longer working well. It seems as if I have read everything before, that I know what the author is going to say before the author has said it. I have lost my pleasure in the path, in the plot, in the tone. This is serious. I cannot substitute broad jumping, or knitting, or baking, for the place that reading held, for the way that reading kept me together. I may just have to allow myself to fly apart until I can read again, the way I am accustomed to.

· · ·

I have to decide but I can't decide in the abstract whether
or not I really want a new companion, a new mate, a new
man in my bed. In theory yes, in reality maybe, maybe not.
There are not so many years left in my life that I couldn't
be alone, get used to being alone, even enjoy being alone. I
could make my work the center of my life. I could make my
children and my grandchildren the center of my life. My
friends could amuse me, hold my hand on difficult days.
This I think would be dignified, proper, reasonable. I could
do this and may have to do this. But then I am having lunch
with a friend who tells me that last night she and her husband, who has Parkinson's disease, who is eighty-two years
old, decided they did not want to go out for dinner and so
they ordered in Japanese food from a good place and they
sat on their couch and watched the movie they had ordered
from Netflix. "We had a great evening," she said. I felt a
wrenching stab of jealousy. H. and I had evenings like that
all the time. There is nothing great about food and a movie
if you are alone in front of the TV. The blue light flickers,
the characters do what they do, the camera zooms about,
but the couch is not a safe haven and the food tastes of card-
board containers and the hours of the evening do not fly by.
Therefore I do want a new companion.

A friend tells me to be careful. You don't want to end
up taking care of an old man you hardly know, with whom
you have shared so little of your life. That is true; however,
it seems too calculating and self-protective to think of that.
She draws it out for me. "If you have a relationship now it
will end very soon at the doctor's office, with you pushing a wheelchair, filling prescriptions, calling for an ambulance, waiting in hospital waiting rooms. You will end up

as a nurse or a social worker filling out forms." There are of course many worse ways to end up. One could be an old crone the children on the block are afraid of when they see you coming down the street. One could be a mad-woman who talks to herself and lives in memories of better times. One could forget how to care for another person. One could be sitting in front of the TV eating takeout food and suffer a final heart attack and days pass before someone misses you. I told H. I would take care of him until I was ninety and then I would run off with the mailman. I didn't get the chance.

This leads to two equally valid questions. Would the mailman want to run off with me and can I still run off with anyone?

．　　．　　．

I have overpaid on H.'s Capital One credit card. Not by a little but by nearly $1,000. I misread the amount owed and overlooked the minus sign and thought the credit was ac-tually a balance. I paid and paid for months, repeating this error. I did not ask myself how the amount could grow, since H. was dead. I did not actually realize that the card was in his name, not mine. I did not ask myself what it was that I was charging. I just assumed that I owed the amount that was actually owed me. Then I noticed and I called. Of course I didn't get a person, not for a long time, not until I held the phone to my ear for over thirty min-utes. I explained. I explained again to an account supervi-sor. I gave all my pertinent information twice. I gave H.'s Social Security number and his mother's maiden name. I waited. They promised a refund check that should arrive after three weeks. It didn't arrive. I forgot about it. Then they send me a bill on his account with a zero balance and I wonder about my check. Again I call and I wait and I speak to two young women who refer me to a third and at last they promise to send the check out again and not to the address on the card, which was his office, where no one is forwarding his mail anymore, but directly to me. I feel strange. I have closed his account. His mail is no longer coming to me. I no longer receive the psychoanalytic journals I used to read each month or the giveaway professional magazines.

·   ·   ·

I wonder about my daughters. Since they are grown people, am I still necessary in their lives? I would hope not. I would hope so. At this point it is my need for them that is the stronger need. I suppress the impulse to call them in the morning, to call them as the day ends. I don't want them to know that I am a cloud hanging above their days. What kind of a mother would allow that? I know them so well that a shift up or down in voice tells me about their state of mind. I hear fatigue. I can tell when something has gone wrong, perhaps seriously, perhaps not. I know them so well that I know that it is time for me to step back, grow a little deaf, allow them to collide with each other, with their children, with their work. This was easier when H. was here. We could talk together about them. We did talk about them incessantly. H. would reassure me if I was worried. He trusted their ability to swim to any shore. Now my love runs in circles, dances around the telephone, waits for it to ring, hangs above my head, bringing most terrible "what if" thoughts in its wake. In fact my daughters are passionate, emotional, caring, nurturing, decent enough people. What more could a mother want? Maybe that they be spared. Spared what? I could make a list but it would be so long that night would fall before I finished and the gates of hell would open and swallow me live.

I want to tell one of my daughters a new thought that has occurred to me about my brother. These days I am always thinking about my dead brother. My nephew is not speaking to me because I hinted in a memoir that his father might have been gay. My nephew, nineteen at the time, thought that by writing about his father, even so delicately, I was not protecting him or considering his response to such news. He accused me of lying. He said I was wrong. He had every right to be angry with me. I was likely more concerned about my book than about his response, although I was not blind to that matter. I worried about my nephew. I wasn't sure what to do. Once I had learned that my brother had a hidden life I could not lie in a published memoir.

H. and I argued. My brother's secret, which he had kept from his son and which I only found out about after his death of AIDS some thirteen years ago, should or should not be told to my nephew. H. thought he was entitled to know. H. thought my nephew should not spend his life without understanding the great family secret that had surrounded his childhood. I wasn't so sure. What if he hated me later? What if he was shaken off his own life course by this information? I suspect there was no good answer. He should know. He shouldn't know. Did he already know? H. and I consulted with two psychoanalysts. They both were very clear that my nephew should have all the information that I had. But psychoanalysts spend their lives uncovering secrets. They are by profession the archenemy of the secret. I wasn't sure. It wasn't my obligation to tell my nephew, but if I didn't who would? I settled on a compromise. I hinted at how my brother contracted AIDS in a few sentences in the last pages of a memoir. Either my nephew would notice or he would not.

He noticed. His mother emphatically denied the fact. Either she was lying or she didn't know. I wasn't sure. My nephew did hate me. He did not speak to me or his cousins after the publication of that memoir. Now ten years later he speaks to one of my daughters. After H.'s death his mother suddenly told him the truth. Yes, his father was gay and had affairs with men from the time my nephew was two years old. Yes, she had always known. What mysterious compromises people make. I understand nothing.

I tell myself that many men have wives and children and frequent gay bars, have male lovers and live double lives. My brother knew a million jokes, spoke four languages fluently, was a hematologist who worked in a lab, was a pianist of considerable quality. He hated football and baseball and psychoanalysis and fresh air. He had asthma and was allergic to dogs and cats and flowers and trees and exercise. He loved Proust and Thomas Mann. I visited him often in the last year of his life. I hoped he was happy to see me but I was never sure. After he died I was going to write a book about a hero scientist who cut himself in his laboratory and got AIDS and died. I went to Montefiore Hospital intending to pick up his published papers on sickle cell anemia and to talk to the head of the lab. The man told me that my brother could not possibly have contracted AIDS in the lab and that he had been seen leaving a gay strip bar in New Orleans on one of their convention trips, and that he had heard from an old lover of my brother's that he was homosexual and he had several other confirmations of his actual sexual preference.

At that time I considered that this chief hematologist might be protecting his lab from possible lawsuit. I wasn't sure if what he was telling me was or was not true. He also told me that my brother had never liked me. That I did believe.

I could not write the book about a hero scientist if he had not caught the disease in the lab. I couldn't stop thinking it over, his secret, mulling it back and forth. H. would tell me to let it go. I would for a while and then my brother and his life would return again to haunt me. That's when I decided to turn the book that was intended to be about a hero scientist into a memoir about the childhood my brother and I shared.

Family secrets are toxic. That is not in doubt. But revealing them may also release poisons. Guilt, guilt at revealing secrets, exposing others, is a common ailment among certain kinds of writers. I am among them. However, for some of us, guilt is more bearable than silence. If I had stayed silent I would have assented to the shame that in places still follows homosexual identity about, building closets where spacious rooms with grand views should have been. In silence we assent to the cover-up of actual human experience.

Would I write that memoir again, the way I wrote it? Would I risk my nephew's fury and our lasting connection for it? Was publishing that memoir worth never meeting my great-niece who bears the female version of my brother's name, and must be two by now? There are no second chances in real life. Even so I suspect I would do it again, just the same way, because many people worship at the feet of one false god or another and the least I can do is be faithful to mine. Guilt is mine ever after.

But now that H. is dead I feel the loss of my only nephew more strongly. Stubbornly, in the face of the facts, I have always wanted more family, not less. Siblings fight and lose each other over the years. Sometimes they just move away to different coasts of the country. Lonely fathers and mothers are despised and forgotten and left to rot in nursing homes. Sometimes they are despised long before their old age. Perhaps we live too long, outlast our connections to our children, place too high a burden on public finance.

I am obsessed now with my brother. It is not that I am thinking new thoughts. It is that I am thinking the same thoughts over and over again. I am overwhelmed by a compulsion to tell everyone I meet about my brother, about his AIDS, about how I should have known before I knew. I speak to an old friend who lives in another city and I tell her the entire story. I am like the Ancient Mariner grasping at the lapels of the wedding guests. I see in people's eyes, as they listen to me, a certain embarrassment, a certain withdrawal; she is quite mad, they think. They are also interested in my tale.

I think about my brother's wife and how she kept his secret and why she kept his secret. I walk along Broadway thinking about him. I sit in my chair in front of the evening news and I think about him. I go over the details of his death in my mind again and again. I know enough to become suspicious of my own tenacious thoughts. Why can't I let him go? Why am I rubbing this sore until it bleeds again and again? When my daughter speaks of my brother's son, my nephew (she's seen him at this party, she had dinner with him here or there, he is doing this or that), I feel guilt like slivers of glass in my spine. I betrayed my brother. I hurt his child. When I imagine how much he would have hated me for that, I grow afraid as if his hate could reach out from the grave and pull me in.

Is it easier to think of my brother, guilt and all, than about H., who should never have left me alone?

. . . .

A seventy-six-year-old man on Match.com sends me his profile. He lives in a suburb of Albany. He is a big man with a mustache and he has a dog on his lap. He says he likes cooking and politics and animals. He says he is conservative, but I am not so opinionated as I used to be. I e-mail him back. I tell him the miles that lie between our cities may prevent any good coming from this meeting. He e-mails me back, "Don't worry about the geography, let's just see what happens." And so I begin. It is absurd to be hopeful from a photo and an e-mail. But I am. He tells me he is a lapsed Catholic. He went to a military Catholic high school and then to a liberal arts college in the West, known for producing hippies and bakers of their own bread. He was divorced twice. He sends me a long piece he has written about his dogs, a poodle mix named Tina and a kind of beagle named Cashew. Tina has died, and he tells me about her death and the way the dog pressed against his thigh in her last hours. He describes disciplining the animals and I see that he is firm but gentle. He lets the neighborhood children play with his dogs. He says that he is interested in spiritual growth. He has had some Jungian therapy. He has also benefited from est. This is not my school of therapy. The sixties rolled off the back of my psychoanalyst medical school husband, and while he was not a conformist Freudian he held no brief for all the shortcuts and the primal screams and soaking in hot tubs and crawling through tunnels to be reborn, which prevailed across the country in wave after wave of self-improvement efforts. I am a very non–New Age person. Put more correctly, I am a very old-age person. But this could be interesting, I tell myself. After all there are many ways to skin a cat and I have respect for anyone who wants to make themselves more conscious, more aware, more capable of surviving in this harsh world.

He sends me a recipe for the black bean soup he is making for dinner. I will not use it, because I'm still calling the local Chinese takeout for dinner, but I print it out anyway and slip it into the worn and tattered, binder split cookbook that H. used most often.

·   ·   ·

I take the subway out to Brooklyn. I remember the Ezra Pound poem: Faces in the subway like petals on a branch. But the faces are not like petals, they are more like bicycle pedals, worn, dark, shadowed, concealing their histories behind a veneer of dust and soot. My face too must look like an old rubber boot left at the bottom of the closet many winters ago. The subway stops running because of a power

outage. We wait in the tunnel a long time. We finally pull
into a station and everyone is asked to exit. I walk to the
surface and find a taxi that crosses the Brooklyn Bridge, oh
brilliant blue water, masts of sailboats that are now docked
at a museum's edge, and in the distance a glimpse of the
Statue of Liberty, her garish green color, like a lady dressed
in another century's fashion, catches the sun's rays. The ca-
bles and the beams of the bridge form a web in the sky. A
police car waits at the entrance of the bridge to catch a ter-
rorist but how can the policeman now drinking his coffee
prevent the pushing of a button, the blowing up of a minivan? How would anyone know a moment before what will
follow? There is the watchtower of the Jehovah's Witnesses.
The route goes by the federal prison and the courthouse. I
arrive at the home of one daughter only a short while after
I was expected.

And then there is my granddaughter. Here love rises,
irrational love, reasonless love. It turns me pink and makes
me wish that H. were there to see the child do only what
all children do but bring me wonder without end. The
child uses a marker on a paper, moves it in almost a circle,
a doll is dropped from the back of a chair, a tower of blocks
grows by my feet. I would sweep the child into my arms
and hold her in my lap. But the child is a moving child, not
a lap child, at least not at this moment. I watch.

When I come home, the subways running again, I slide
into my chair and open my e-mail. My correspondent has
sent me a very long article about peace in the Middle East.
It is about the eternal treachery of Arabs and the vile prem-
ises of the Muslim religion. I do not agree. I do not like
this view. But I assume that because this man knows I am

Jewish he is bending over, perhaps too far, to protect my interests as he perceives them. I take the article as an offering of friendship. I am far more moderate in my views and hopeful of reconciliations that may not come but must still be hoped for, if sanity is to be maintained.

The question arises again: am I capable of a new love? Or is it gone, that willingness to open my mind to another, even more alarming, to let the hand of another go between my thighs or rest lightly on my breasts? I lie down on my couch and listen to Ray Charles. I am old but he was blind and that didn't stop him. He would understand my moment of unreasonable, unsubstantiated optimism.

· · ·

The form comes from the monument makers. There is a sketch of the stone with H.'s name on it. Under his name and his date of birth and his date of death I have told them to put the words HUSBAND, FATHER, GRANDFATHER AND PHYSICIAN. The words are there on the design, on the right side of the tablet. On the left there is a blank space, for my name and any additional words my children will choose. The ground under my side of the stone is still undisturbed. Perhaps I will take a course at the Museum of Natural History and find out the names of the strata of earth, the mineral and rock that lie beneath. I am supposed to approve the sketch and sign the bottom of the page. Also I am to include a very substantial check. I stare at the blank space. I am cowering like Scrooge on the visitation of Christmas Future. Only no behavior change, no reform of my bad character, no effort to improve my mortal soul can affect the sentence. I consider telling the children what words I want carved onto my side of the stone. But they would be angry at my morbid thought. I'll let them make up their own words; after all I won't know or care. Being dead grants someone else the final word.

So I sign the form and place it in the envelope provided and put the stamp on the corner. One of these days I will even mail it.

· · ·

I go with a couple I have known for many years to a fine Indian restaurant. The walls are covered in red velvet. We walk in under the drapes of brightly patterned tent with golden tassels binding up the fabric. We drink, we talk, we order food. Strange food, hot and spicy and sweet and cool to the lips, tikkas, tandoori lamb and chicken, naans, raitas, samosas. Old friends, we talk about people we know, we talk about the president of the United States. We pause to think of the war so far away. We talk about our children, what they are doing. We talk about our exercise classes. They talk about trips they are going to take to faraway places. I am enjoying this meal, these friends, this evening. When I return to my apartment and turn on the light and listen to the cat purring his usual welcome, I am not surprised that I am alone in the apartment. I look directly into the mirror and see my face. For the first time in months I do not turn my eyes away. Perhaps it's the wine but perhaps not.

· · ·

Islands of ice on the Hudson River and above them a heavy fog hangs. The water and the sky are the same color and impossible to tell where one ends and the other begins. Over on the other side I can barely distinguish the high hills that line the shore and the apartment houses that stand there with their multileveled parking garages and their small terraces. I have dinner with two friends after a movie. He has had thyroid cancer, she has had breast cancer. They both seem well and we discuss the covenant with God, and how to maintain it in the absence of faith. We discuss how it was possible for her parents, loyal Communists until the day they died, to have excused the Gulag and the purges and the famines and the murders of so many. "Hope," my friend explains. She loved her mother and her father. "Lunacy," says her husband, and I agree. We leave the restaurant and find a coating of white snow on the street outside. My friends hail a passing taxi and disappear, two heads together in the backseat. Snow is falling. I open my mouth to let the flakes fall on my tongue. This is not a dignified thing for a woman of my age to be doing. A man passes wrapped in scarves. He looks at me startled. I close my mouth.

Once, forty-six years ago in a snowstorm I had walked many blocks alone in deep drifts to the hospital to give birth to my first child. I was in my first marriage. I was twenty-four. I was carrying a typewriter back from the repair shop when my water broke. This is a memory that will disappear the instant I die, as my neurons will quickly shrivel and the synapses turn to dry proteins. It has no significance outside my brain. But now it fills my mind, the leaping forward of my life as my first child was placed in my arms, as I stood in the hospital room looking out the window at the park covered with white mounds of snow, the window streaked with blurred flakes, the ground pockmarked with the boot steps of passersby.

. . .

When I am alone all day, have gone nowhere, have spoken to no one, after it turns dark I remember the way it was when I was a child and I had a sickness. I was prone to ear infections, coughs and the usual disasters of childhood. My mother was afraid to enter a sick child's room. She was afraid of germs and of doing something wrong that might harm the child. She would stand at the door and wave good-bye to me in the morning and good-night in the evening. The nanny who attended to such needs would bring me lunch on a tray and medicine when it was time but did not stay to play a game of cards or teach me how to knit. Sometimes, being sick, I would sleep, curled up, my head on the pillows. Sometimes I would play with whatever interested me at the moment. But mostly I read, and I read. My mother would send books into the room with the maid who lived in the little room in our apartment next to the cook's behind the pantry. The days had a particular length, like no other days. The hours moved slowly. My pajamas became stained with food. My hair was tangled. I lingered over the last pages of the last book I had. What would I do when they were all read? How would the time pass? The evening darkness meant supper on a tray would soon arrive.

Now sometimes that comes back to me: the same sensation, the same slowness of time, the same unmarked hours. H. is not returning in the evening. I talk to a friend on the phone. I call one of my daughters. I try to read. I write. Still the time is sluggish, the shadows persistent and unfriendly.

NOW I AM RECEIVING E-MAILS AT THE RATE OF THREE A DAY from my new Albany friend from Match.com. He sends me more soup recipes. He sends me a photograph of himself and four or five other children age around seven or eight. I look in the child's eyes. The boy is wearing suspenders. There are a few girls in the photograph. They wear the flower print dresses of another era. Their hair is curled and pinned with bows. He sends me another photograph of himself, now grown, standing on a scrubby mound with brush about his feet and a low-rising mountain in the bleak distance. He has a long rifle over his shoulder and an army coat that comes down to his ankles and a cigarette dangling out of the corner of his mouth. The photograph is labeled in bold letters, KOREA. That is the way we make our men. There is an arrogance in his posture. I like that. I am interested in that and in the size of him, as if no wind could knock him down. Several hours later another photograph appears on my computer. This one is of a man about thirty or is it forty, in profile, smoking, and the smoke rises upwards as if the photo were taken in a jazz club, or at a party, or in the midst of a conversation about the meaning of life. Ah, he is trying to seduce me with an old photo of the way he was once. This is ridiculous. But effective. After all we are not suddenly seventy—or rather our seventy is an accumulation of all the other ways we were, our five-year-old selves became our ten-year-old selves and so on and on and if we unpack our souls the whole album appears and every

moment is a part of the following moment and we are all
a continuum that includes all the ways we were that we
have forgotten. Anyway that is my excuse for staring and
staring at this photograph that does not lead me directly
to the man who is e-mailing me, but is tantalizing nevertheless.

· · ·

Perhaps we should talk on the phone, he says in an e-mail.
We agree on a time, a day later.

He has sent me some strange e-mails. He seems to be on
the Web gathering pieces from right-wing commentators.
He sends me an article claiming that the weapons of mass
destruction were in Iraq but that the delay at the United
Nations allowed Saddam Hussein to take them all into Syria
for safekeeping. A few hours later I receive another e-mail,
on the inadequacy of the public school system and the need
for vouchers and choice. I am not willing to argue about
that. It is followed by an article against affirmative action.
Which is followed by a piece on the bell curve and the
lack of intrinsic intelligence in African-Americans. This is
disturbing. I do not respond. "Why," his next e-mail says,
"are you not debating me? Why are you not coming up
with counterarguments?" I answer, "Do you want a debating partner or a friendship?" He responds with a report
on his trip to the nearby market, which has foods from
all over the world on its shelves. He tells me he can cook
a fine chicken Marabella. I think of it, this big man, with
his almost-beagle dog waiting in the car, which is parked
in a large lot at the mall. I see him in the aisles pushing
his cart, gathering his spices together. I think of walking

alongside him on this shopping trip. I don't bother to read the entire next e-mail that arrives. It is about the implacable hatred expressed in the Koran and the basic evil that underlies all Muslim thought. I've heard this before. I am suddenly exhausted. Has my blood pressure dropped to a dangerous low?

I ignore his e-mail about the Koran. I don't bother to tell him what cruel and immoral deeds can be found in our very own Bible. I don't want to fight. I have something else in mind. He sends me an e-mail about the lack of patriotism among members of the Democratic Party. I send him back an e-mail and tell him I'm going to the movies with friends. Within moments he sends me an e-mail that says the *New York Times* prints only lies about Republicans and slants the news away from the truth. I don't answer. I have my winter coat on, my scarf is around my neck. I will be late if I don't leave immediately.

I turn off my computer.

· · · ·

How important are world events between a man and a woman? I suppose it depends on how passionate the two partners are about their political convictions. I am not indifferent or even cool. I am not a woman who normally can leave it alone and turn the conversation to the children or the school situation, or the economic news. I am more like a dog who must dig up every bone in the garden and gnaw it again and again, leaving the flower bed uprooted and worms crawling across every surface. But I tell myself that people have reasons for their beliefs. Perhaps his fierce ones are a sign of caring, not a sign of a fondness for authority and a respect for guns learned in childhood, a very different childhood than mine. I remind myself that I have known contributors to the campaign to exile snowmobiles from national parks who are cruel to their daughters and leave their wives on the equivalent of an ice floe in the Antarctic.

·   ·   ·

I lose my leather gloves. I always lose my gloves. Each winter I promise myself one pair only and each winter I need more. I stop in a store on Broadway to replace the lost pair. I have a moment of financial panic. I can't do this. I can't just buy gloves as if money were infinite, could be wasted on a whim because I am careless and distracted. I look at the gloves on the glass counter, smooth, soft gloves. I could just as easily have thrown away twenty-dollar bills as lost my gloves. People work hard for their money. I am ashamed of myself. When H. was alive I let him worry about waste and prudence and caution. I laughed at him for his miserly, Depression-born ways. But now I have lost the silver spoon I was born with. Now I have to be responsible.

But not that responsible. I can afford another pair of gloves. I will be able to pay the bills even if I lose my coat, my scarf, my boots and need to replace them all. This is a game I am playing with myself. Money is not the real subject. The poverty I fear is the poverty of soul that is mine. I buy the gloves. I promise myself to take good care of them. I forgive myself for the fact that I am not always clear on where the pain is coming from and what to do to stem its onslaught.

·   ·   ·

I had spent the day before making a soup for a Sunday brunch. I had chopped and peeled and bought cheese and smoked salmon. I was worried that my soup was too spicy. I was worried that I could not, not without H., bring the food to the table, open the wine bottles, brew the coffee. Then at night I had a terrible nightmare. In my dream I was somewhere out of town, somewhere where the trains were not running and no taxis stopped, and I needed to return to the city because I was expecting people to come to my house for lunch. How terrible it would be if I were not there. If they rang the bell and no one answered the door. My anxiety mounted, my heart pounded, as I saw the clocks in the town square and realized that I did not have time to return even if the trains began to run again. And then I was sitting on a bench and four people approached me. One of them was a strange woman. The others were lawyers with briefcases. The woman said, "We are going to sue you and take everything you have. You will be left with nothing." A great panic swept over me. I woke up with a splitting headache.

My rational mind scolded my overheated brain for such a stupid nightmare. But then it came to me. Everything I had was gone. Everything that mattered to me had been taken. H. was gone. I was stripped bare. The dream was not a threat but a report. Of course, the "everything" here is an exaggeration, hyperbole, absurdity. I have my children and grandchildren. I have my work. I have my apartment with its books and its drawings and its furniture H. and I bought together. I have my photos and my memories and I have friends. I have, at least for now, my health. I have my cat. So it's not accurate to say I have lost every-

thing. I will not indulge in melodrama, at least not for
long.

My soup was a success. It was not too spicy. It was just
right. But in the next night I had another dream. The
phone rang and I had trouble picking it up. It fell out of
my hands. Finally after many attempts I put the phone
to my ear. It was H. "I stumbled," he said. "Are you all
right?" I asked. I saw a great ravine and a river running
beneath high rocks. He was on a trip. "Are you all right?"
I repeated. He answered me, but I couldn't understand his
answer. I woke up. My pillow was soaking wet. He had
stumbled up the steps to our lobby moments before he lost
consciousness. If this were the century of séances and para-
normal experiences I would believe he had been trying to
contact me from beyond the grave. What I believed was
that I had allowed his voice to return to my head. I had
brought back his dying moment because I could. It did
not shatter me. It was just a dream.

· · ·

A psychoanalyst friend tells me that soon memories of H.
will come to comfort me. He will be like an imaginary
friend, a companion of my thoughts. I find that idea uncomfortable. It has a Hallmark-card quality. The odor of
false witness is in the air. I remember the tie he wore to our
daughter's wedding when I see it on his tie rack. I remember the way he pushed back tears with his hands when we
thought another daughter was going to die of pneumonia.
I remember how he chopped onions at our kitchen table.
I remember how he lifted a child up to feed the goats at
the zoo. I am not comforted by these memories. I simply

remember. He is not hanging in the air beside me, a voice whispering in my ear. He is not telling me to return to work. He is not going through the refrigerator throwing out moldy cheese. He is not watching over me, as the song says. He is not.

. . .

So now at the arranged time my new friend from Albany calls. He has a deep voice. Just the voice I imagined. He tells me that we need an antiballistic system and must break our treaties in order to develop one. The Chinese and the North Koreans will destroy us if we don't. I disagree but I don't want to argue politics. "Tell me about your childhood," I say.

And he does. He grew up in Trenton, New Jersey, one of eight children. His grandfather arrived here from a far corner of the Austro-Hungarian Empire and carried cement in large wheelbarrows to the construction workers on the scaffolding above. His father owned a bakery and was working all the time. His mother was bitter and never hugged a child. He was small-boned and slight and was always being beaten up by the other boys. His childhood was full of pain. I could imagine this boy on the streets of Trenton, the soot of factories in the air, the hardness of his mother's life, the lack of play and tenderness. He told me he went to a Catholic military school. I hadn't known there was such a thing. "I wore a uniform," he says. "But the boys still beat me up." Now he is six foot two but when he graduated high school he was just a bit over five feet. "How did you grow so many inches after high school?" I ask. "I just did," he says. We stop talking; the conversation

has gone on a long time. I like his voice. I like the gruff-
ness of it.

The next morning I receive two e-mails from him
about the takeover of European culture by the immigrant
Arabs. It is predicted that in twenty-five years Notre Dame
will become a mosque and the Louvre will be closed down.
I don't argue. How can one argue such a point? Where to
start? I put the e-mail out of my mind. I notice a lightness
in my spirit as I race toward the phone when it rings at the
time we have arranged.

As I talk to him I sit in my favorite place in the apartment where I can see the Empire State Building over the
rooftops. The sun is slipping down across the river. I can
see the clouds above, growing pink with the approaching
evening. I lean back in the chair and the cat jumps on my
chest. With one hand I hold the phone to my ear, with the
other I stroke the cat. "Why did you get divorced?" I ask
and he tells me. A long time ago, in a suburban county of
New York, he lived with his wife and three children. He
had a best friend and the best friend had a wife and the
four of them had dinner together often and their children
played together. It was the early seventies. His wife was in
therapy. One evening she told him the truth. She had been
having an affair with his best friend. He moved out. He
tried psychotherapy for a few weeks but it didn't work out.

It was a time of chaos. Homes were breaking up everywhere. Women were leaving to discover themselves as
potters or dancers. No one wanted to miss out on living to
the fullest, discovering yourself. The discipline of family
life seemed like a yoke on an ox's shoulder. No one wanted
to be the ox. My friend on the phone begins to talk about

the damage that feminism did to the American home. I remind him that the American family was less than perfect before girls went to medical school. I ask him about the neighborhood where he lives now. He tells me about the store where he shops for Asian spices. I see him in my mind's eye. He wears the big hat that I saw in his photo. His grocery cart is filled. His dog is waiting for him in the car, nose pressed to the glass. I think to myself that he was hurt by his wife's betrayal and I hope, a thin, wispy hope, a hope that could, if I were otherwise inclined, be the beginnings of a prayer. Could I make whole what had been torn asunder? Could I provide the balm for what still burned? His children, he tells me, were permanently harmed by the divorce, because his wife was unable to provide the discipline that the children needed. One boy disappeared into a world of drugs. She was working. She was not strong enough. He told her that. But she ignored him. He talks of other connections, a second wife who disappointed him quickly, a liberal woman who sent him e-mails for over two years.

The sky is now gray. Smoke from an incinerator a few blocks away is rising black toward the pale star that hangs above it. I have to be at a friend's house for dinner in a half hour. I end the conversation. "Good night," I say. "Until tomorrow," he says, and I can hear my heart ready to race forward. I go to dinner like a teenager with an invitation to the prom secure in my possession.

·   ·   ·

"I have the perfect person to introduce you to," says a friend. "Yes," I say. "There is a problem though," she adds. "Yes,"

I say. "He is a prominent lawyer. You know his name. He was in the Clinton administration." She tells me his name. I recognize it. His wife has died. "He told me he wants to find somebody," my friend says. "What is the problem?" I ask. I imagine the answer. He has early Alzheimer's. He has liver cancer. He is going to jail for some white-collar crime that was reported in the business section of the *New York Times*, which I keep meaning to read but don't. She says, "He is exactly your age, but he wants a much younger woman." "Oh, that," I say. I shrug. I smile. I'm not surprised. I just forget from time to time that I have faded from the field. "I could introduce you," she says, "maybe he would change his mind." "No thank you," I say.

My cousin lives in a gated community built around a beautiful golf course, in Boca Raton. He is seventy-eight years old and divorced several times. He told me that in his community if a woman turns fifty she is considered beyond the pale. I believe him. He told me that he didn't want to date a woman in her sixties, because in no time at all he would spend his days driving her to doctors. There is a toughness in that statement that surprises me in my sweet cousin but I suspect that the moving sewage that streams between men and women, the misogyny, the fear, the neediness, the rage, the helplessness, the lust, the failure of lust, of one or the other partner, creates such a stink that it's a wonder anyone can cross the river to the other side. And people do. I see that they do it.

· · ·

Some days now I feel calm and content, content for hours at a time. Some days I sink again. I lose interest in everything.

I mope. I do not admire moping. Nevertheless I mope.

I hear from a doctor friend of mine that people who try to commit suicide by taking various sleeping pills, tranquilizers, antianxiety drugs, aspirin, whatever they can glean from their medicine cabinets, most often end up in hospitals, with stroke, with paralysis, with brain damage but alive and condemned to years of confinement to a nursing home. I wonder if this is true. Is it possible that this is just a way doctors have of warning us not to try to escape our lives? Like prison guards, they point to electrified fences. Who dares to test them? I don't know how to check this information casually, without revealing my intense and personal interest in the subject. I know about the Hemlock Society but I find their recommendation of a plastic bag over one's head almost impossible to imagine. It's like putting your hand in the fire: wouldn't you withdraw it at the first flush of pain? I wish I knew a doctor who would inoculate his patient with air if the time had truly come. But whose decision would that be? How many people jump to their deaths, either literally or figuratively, who six months later would be eating pasta at their favorite Italian restaurant with a new love in their lives if someone had only stayed their hand at the moment of momentary desperation? Some people kill themselves too soon. Some people kill themselves too late. I hope I will have the courage to act when I should act and the courage not to act if I shouldn't.

I would ask my stepdaughter the physician to tell me the most efficient way to die but she would never give me an answer. She knows the answer. On any other subject I know she would tell me all she knows. On this subject she would not. She is a physician and sworn to do no harm even if harm would be doing good. Also she loves me. A complicated love, affected by torn loyalties, to be sure, but a love nevertheless. Does she love me enough to help me escape? Or does she love me too much to help me escape?

It would be inexcusable of me to put her in that vise. One does not squeeze one's child, not ever. After all, I love her too.

.   .   .

Sometimes at night in bed I imagine sex, the kind we had, all the kinds we had. I discover that I have available in my brain images that suffice, will do. I am glad of this. It is not as good as the real event, as the real heat, sweat, rub and wear and tear of human part with human part. But it is reassuring to know that it has not gone from me, not all the way.

.   .   .

I think of the goddess Diana, mistress of the moon, mistress of the hunt, a dog by her side, a quiver of arrows hanging from her shoulder. In the modern city there is no Diana, there is no shrine built to appease her in the parks, there is no game for her to hunt. All that is left is the moon going on its way like the subways on their tracks. If I believed in Diana then I would believe in the underworld, a place across the river Styx where the dead floated without purpose through the remainder of time and I could imagine myself there possibly finding a shade I once had loved.

.   .   .

I read a book, at last I can read an entire book, in a reasonable number of hours. The book is a memoir by a young woman who finds God in an ashram in India. Good for her. Not for me. Western culture has eaten my heart and there seems to be very little I can do about it.

· · ·

Sometimes I do wish I could transcend myself. I see H.'s gloves on the closet floor. In the outdoors–survival stores he searched for the thickest, warmest gloves he could find, because he had Reynaux's disease, which turned his fingertips and toes blue in the cold. He said he wouldn't die of it and he didn't. But the disease caused him to wear double pairs of socks and thick black Thermasil gloves that were less than elegant. I see them now behind my summer sandals where they must have fallen months ago, and I feel a love uncontainable, a love for his fingers and his toes and his blood vessels that were not as competent as they should be. I feel his heavy-gloved hand as it tucks my windblown hair back behind my ear. His absence is for a flashing moment or two near intolerable and then becomes tolerable again. I might feel like Orpheus, who had lost for the last and final time Eurydice because he turned back to look at her. But I don't. I feel instead a need to get some food in the house. I have forgotten again to buy milk and bread and cereal.

· · ·

I sit down at my computer. It is not yet seven in the morning. I open my Outlook Express and there is another e-mail from my new friend in Albany. This morning he sends me an article on the outrageous conduct of professors in major universities who are silencing views that contradict their own. This may be true. But there is a grinding sound in this article. It reflects a grudge, a bitter bite that has been taken from the apple. I could write back and begin an argument on this but instead I write and say, "Tell me about your children." I receive an e-mail almost immediately. He will call at noon. Noon is not so far away.

·   ·   ·

I am taking a class on ancient history in the land of Israel. I look around the room. I see primarily widows like me, gray hair, wrinkled skin, eyes behind thick glasses or freckled hands with veins raised like a relief map, showing mountains and valleys. I see a young woman with a sad face, stringy hair, no makeup, work boots; I see a middle-aged woman wearing a turban over what is likely a bare scalp. There are two men in the class. One is young and his hands are trembling. Medication, I think. The other is old and sweet and his mind creaks. Words escape him, meanings elude him, but he is there and always greets me with a smile that exposes his worn-out, crooked teeth. I am learning. I do the reading carefully. I am excited by the visions that come into my head. I am understanding something that was previously mysterious. There are exiles and captivities, and wars and emperors exacting tribute and kings that fall and kings that rise.

Why does this matter to me now? Why have I chosen this class? The city is full of opportunity for learning. I could do pottery. I could become a photographer. I could learn about medieval sculpture or Asian jewelry. I could find out about political theory or the development of Third

World countries. Knowledge of all things is available to me. But this is what I wanted.

Also I wanted to leave my apartment. I wanted to do something I had not done before. I wanted to move forward into new territory both social and of the mind. But why ancient Biblical history?

The strangeness of the stories interests me but the familiarities comfort me. If it has always been the way it is now, then perhaps it will always be: something continues, someone returns from exile, someone plants a new orchard, someone holds a newborn baby. The conqueror comes, the conqueror falls. The long line of human error is oddly soothing. I read in Jeremiah, "My bowels, my bowels! I am pain at my very heart, my heart maketh a noise in me: I cannot hold my peace because thou hast heard, O, my soul, the sound of the trumpet, the alarm of war." I see it on the news each night.

I like my class. I like my fellow students. It is good at the end of your life to imagine the beginnings of history. The more I know of history the easier it will be to release my dear (dear to me) little soul into the eons, when the time comes.

· · ·

I wake in the morning with my head pounding and my heart racing. There is no good reason for this. I feel over-excited, as if I am about to dive from a ridiculous height into a small barrel. Is it hormones that have no business running amok in my body at this time of my life? Is it a reaction to a nightmare that I can't remember? Is it anxiety because I notice again that I wake in bed alone and I sleep alone? This is not a surprise. This is not a shock. It should not make my heart shake in my chest. Perhaps I am ill. But with what? I could call the doctor. Instead I take two Advil and wait for calm to return. Perhaps it is the taxes? I have an appointment with my accountant this afternoon. May the god of widows protect me from the government, leave me some spare change.

• • •

So I receive ten more e-mails in twenty-four hours from my friend in Albany. The phone rings at the appointed hour and we talk. He wants me to clean up my computer and he walks me through the process, giving me instructions in his deep, gruff voice. Oddly I feel as if we are dancing with one another as I press the key that he tells me to and then click and click again on my computer. He advises new software. He advises updates. I agree but don't write down the names of the many additions he claims I need. I am dancing with my eyes closed. This is all right. Then I ask him again about his children. There is a deep sigh on the other end of the phone. My daughter, he explains, and begins a long story that is somewhat incomprehensible, probably because he isn't telling me all, and possibly because he doesn't understand it. His wife poisoned his relationship with the children. The daughter in high school began to talk to him on the phone and they became close. When she went to college he talked to her every day about her mind, her soul, her friends, his politics, his life, his Jungian theories, his belief in possible reincarnation. He was a part of everything she did and thought. And then she went to medical school and became a doctor and suddenly she pulled away and wouldn't take his phone calls. Then she got married and she had two children and she wouldn't let him see the children. He had never met them. "Why?" I asked. "What happened?" "She sent me a Christmas card last year," he replied, "but I told her I didn't want her cards. It was torture to see the photos of the children I am not allowed to meet." "But what happened?" I asked. He did not answer. I think perhaps he was too much, too overbearing, too strong a force—or perhaps there was a history of something worse. I put that thought out of my mind.

I am thinking of inviting him down to stay with me for a few days. I imagine him driving down and bringing Cashew, his dog, the almost-beagle with sad eyes. I imagine him parking his car on my street. I imagine the terror my cat would feel on seeing his dog. I ask a good friend who lives a few blocks away whether she would take my cat for a few days if I have a visiting friend with a dog. "No," she says.

·   ·   ·

I am invited to hear a pianist friend play in her home with a violinist she knows. I accept. The musicians play Beethoven's "Kreutzer Sonata," No. 9. The violinist has a harsh but passionate tone but the pianist is perfect. I see her bending over the keys, looking somewhat like a painting of a nineteenth-century farm lady, shy, unassuming, colored like a sparrow, but underneath it all, the swells and dips of the music dominate, hint at bliss, promise more, withdraw the promise, pierce, roll forward, hurt even in its gentleness. My muscles, my veins, my tendons, my organs all respond. I sit on a chair in a living room where I had been so often with H. and I don't think of him, I listen, listen as if I were

an ear, not a mind. Usually I can't hear music without in-
truding thoughts, observations, memories, words and more
words, arriving uninvited. I wonder if I have changed, if
the white water of grief has not worn out my critical, observing, commenting mind and left me smoother, like a
blanket tucked in by a loving mother. After the music there
is supper and instantly I return to my chattering self, my
storytelling self, my excited-by-the-whiff-of-a-party self.
But I don't forget what it was like to listen. I promise it
won't be the last time music makes its way through the
jumble of my brain.

This is the home of a psychoanalyst. Artists and poets,
men of medicine, historians and museum curators have
dined here. I look about the room. There are four people
with serious cancers sitting near. Among the guests there
have been more than half a dozen bypass surgeries. I know
of at least one Parkinson's sufferer, who sits in a chair at the
far back. I know of one mother whose child was severely
crippled by cerebral palsy. I know of another whose son is
struggling with autism and a mother whose son is mentally
ill and over on the bench by the Christmas cactus I see a
father whose son is a drug addict and disappeared years ago.
I smile and wave at the married man with a long ponytail
and a gold earring whose mistress of long standing sits near
me. I know of several unmarried childless middle-aged
daughters whose disappointed mothers are standing nearby
holding plates with pasta piled high.

I wonder why, with all the civilization in the room, so
much went wrong, so many regrets hang in the casual gestures, the lifted wineglasses, the discussions of politics and
biology that rise from across the room. Everyone here has

been to Florence and Provence and Madrid and everyone
here knows the names of at least three good restaurants in
Paris. Is it dull of me to notice that sophistication, erudi-
tion, professional success is not a sufficient shield against
the slings and arrows that keep arriving year after year? I
do not believe that psychoanalysts failed their families in
a manner worse or different from other people. I do not
believe that shrinks are like choreographers, ones who can
describe but can't do. Accountants and investment folk,
advertising and marketing people, salespeople and shop-
keepers, basketball coaches and insurance agents have their
sad tales as well. Out the window of this apartment I see
the lamp lights in the park across the street blinking. I can
barely see the dark water of the reservoir, and the stone
wall that binds the park off from the avenue. Should we all
have lived differently? And if so, how? How?

· · ·

Now comes a slew of e-mails, two or three at a time from
my friend from Albany. One is about the need to allow all
citizens to carry handguns when they leave their homes. I
e-mail back, "How are you? Do you like Dickens?" Immediately in reply I receive an e-mail. This one is a long
article—I can hardly make my way through it, although
I try—about the importance of the free market. I agree
that the market should not be controlled by the government, but I'm not sure that means that government should
abandon the health care of poor children or the bettering of
schools. I'm not sure I understand economics well enough
to have firm opinions. If the stock market in Hong Kong
falls, am I in danger of losing my retirement funds and if

so should I put them under my mattress? My e-mail friend does not answer my question on Dickens. Nevertheless I think about his coming to New York. I think about his face. I look again at the boyhood photos he has sent me that I have saved on my computer. I stare and stare.

I tell a friend about him. She is not impressed. "I would cut off all contact," she says. I ignore her. She is passionate about her politics, which are not his, nor mine. "He's probably an anti-Semite," she says. He calls in the late afternoon. I curl up on my couch near a window where I can watch the owl who sits on a high fire escape across the way. "I know," I say, "you are very pro-Israel in your fashion, but what about Jews, Jewish people I mean?" I ask. He says that his second wife was Jewish. They were only married for two years. She thought his father, who was living with them, was anti-Semitic. "Why?" I ask. "Because," he says, "my father hardly talked to her. But that's because he hardly talked. He was old. I took him to live with my brother."

I ask him about his brothers and sisters. Of the eight of them, three are dead, two aren't talking to each other. And he has lost touch with one of the others. That sounds normal to me. I like the low sound of his voice. I lean into it. I ask about Cashew. I tell him about the movie I had seen the night before with friends. We agree to talk the next day. The owl on the fire escape flies away, circles above in the sky and then disappears from view. He must have seen a rat in the park. I feel as if I have a secret, a good small secret deep within. I recognize the feeling from the first weeks of pregnancy, before I dared tell H., before anyone else knew, before it was confirmed by a rabbit who

died for me. I fall asleep easily. I wake up and rise without
(my usual habit) first running my hands over H.'s side of
the bed as if I were confirming his absence.

What do I like here? The voice of the man is deep and
rumbles from inside his chest. He is sure of what he thinks.
He is odd, unconventional, a cook. He has large, sad eyes.
He likes dogs. He is interested in me. He wants to know
more about me. He is so other, so unlike anyone in my life.
This is fine. He is slightly dangerous. Why? I sense it in
his politics. I sense it in his many failed relationships. The
danger should send me in the other direction. It doesn't.
He is appealing like a man who has been in a terrible fight
and wouldn't think of speaking of it. He is romantic—or is
he evil? Is there a point at which these two qualities inter-
sect?

* * *

I am an old lady but I can still flirt, tease, encourage, lead
on, and play. In dancing school, when I was a girl, I learned
that all you had to do to make a boy rush across the floor
to ask you to dance a second time was to inquire about his
favorite sport, to say something respectful about the position he played, to ask him about his summer camp or his
winter vacation. If a boy begins to talk to you he is happy
with you. My mother taught me that. Later is plenty of time
to be yourself, to pick among the boys the one who most
pleases you. The first job is to attract and for that you must
reflect. I wonder if that is still true. My daughters are made
of sterner stuff: perhaps, but perhaps not.

* * *

I receive an e-mail from Albany. It is about the outrageous demand of homosexuals to marry one another. It is about their intent to destroy marriage as an institution. It speaks of their filthy behaviors. Of course millions of people believe this. I, however, have not known any. I try to understand why the love of two men or two women for each other would harm anyone else. I don't. I am repelled by the tone of the piece. It is angry and threatened and disturbed. Disturbed in all senses of the word, I think. Does he believe what he says in this e-mail? Of course he does, why else would he send it to me? Is this because he was raised Catholic, in Catholic schools? Can I ignore this e-mail? I want to. This is not a point that can be argued. No mind is going to be changed by logic or reason on either side. I think of my brother who lived his life with a cover story, with a lie, who was surly and bitter and often in a defensive crouch, or so I thought. Who would he have been if he had walked this earth with his own sexual nature fulfilled in love? H. would be patient with this irrational fear of the sexual other. He would find its source in our own childhood sexual confusions. I am impatient. The tone of the e-mail from Albany is ugly. All day I avoid thinking about it. I go for a walk.

I have lunch with a friend and discuss her husband's newest book and then I go to the dentist and have my teeth cleaned. My mouth is perfect for the moment. And in the evening I sit down to answer the e-mail. I do not present a long argument, although I know that Albany would like that. I just say I disagree. I think marriage is a hard matter, but no affection, no physical need that doesn't cause hurt, is wrong or, if he wishes, ungodly. In fact, I say, if God is anywhere on this planet, He is in the love one human can feel for another, sexual love included. I don't mean pedophiles. This exception weakens my argument but exceptions don't so much prove a rule as erupt like mushrooms on the lawn after a rain. There. I send my e-mail and I go to bed.

I think of all the e-mails I have received from Albany. The worldview is angry, furious even, as if some band of evil spirits had set fire to the Eden that once was home. There is a consistent lack of compassion in all the material, whether the subject is the intelligence of the poor, or the needs of the welfare mother, or the marriage of homosexuals. It is not the point of view that is so disturbing, it is the undercurrent of rage that burns and burns on. Why am I reading all these e-mails? Why am I ignoring what they say about the sender? But perhaps I am being provincial. If I can only have a relationship with a man who thinks as I do I will cut off most of the world. Perhaps I should be patient and see what comes next. I go to my computer. I look again at the photographs of the schoolboy with the suspenders on. I see the man on a hilltop in Korea, a big man, with the stance of a warrior. I see the sad-eyed man smoking a cigarette, a black-and-white photo of a man with a mind—handsome, but that is not the point, it is the brooding darkness, the poignant steam that comes from the lines in the face. Is it fury or sadness I see? I lean over my computer till my nose is almost against the screen. I want to protect this man. I want him to protect me.

I KNOW MY DAUGHTERS WELL, BUT THERE ARE MANY PLACES our conversations do not go, where they would barricade the doors against my entrance. This is fair. Even if I have a god-given right to know everything about them, given the changing of the diapers, the milk from the nipple, the holding of small hands, the pushing on the swing, etc., I renounce that right, in the name of reality. I am willing to settle for a crumb or two, an afternoon of conversation. This is a bond that pulls and pushes at the same time.

My daughters do call but their calls only make me thirst for more. I am greedy for their voices, addicted to their voices. This must stop, I tell myself. This will stop, I tell myself. Time will shift my attention elsewhere, I tell myself. However, at the moment I am staring at the clock. I will call after seven p.m. I will think of something to say, a reasonable reason for the call. Or perhaps I can hold off until tomorrow evening. Or they will call me? They usually do. Do they know how much their calls mean to me? I hope not. I expect so.

. . .

It is the evening of my ancient biblical history class. I set off all wrapped up in my down coat, warm scarf, gray wool gloves. I head up the block, the wind off the river at my back. It is early and people are returning from work, briefcases, tote bags, hurrying along the street. There is a woman with two little girls, holding her hands. There is a man who lives in my building pushing his bike. There are the lights of cars on the avenue, the lights in the rooms around me. There is the black river at my back. I want to turn around and go back to my apartment. I don't. I walk the few blocks along Broadway, past the Chinese-Cuban restaurant now filling up with customers. I hurry by the French bistro where H. always ordered the skate and cross the street in front of the Indian-owned newspaper store that sells lottery tickets. I walk carefully on a narrow path with scaffolding overhead where a new building is rising. At its base security guards are standing. Avoiding the wind, I cling to the walls of the grocery store where I see long lines at the checkout counter. I get on the bus and I want to get off but I don't. I get to my class. I forget myself and the odor of aloneness that follows me around, I am swept into the invading armies from the East and the rebuilding of temples and the forced marches of souls away from their homes. I am alive. I go home content. I order dinner from the Mexican restaurant and I eat it in front of the television. I drink a glass of red wine.

. . .

I send an e-mail to Albany. I have not asked him to visit. I have grown a little cautious. In my e-mail, I write that I think we may be too different from one another. I write that my worldview is not so much to the left of his as somewhere in another universe. I tell him how much I respect him but fear that our relationship has come to an end. He sends me another e-mail. "We will get past this too," he says. "Don't rush to judgment." I am calmed. Perhaps it will be all right. I send an e-mail later that evening with a report on my class and I tell him the names and ages of my children. Hardly an hour has passed and there on my computer is his answering e-mail. He talks of the evil of the homosexuals who took over the seminaries in the 1960s and admitted only homosexuals to their priestly ranks and how they abused little boys and the cover-up that followed and the disgusting behavior of the homosexual priests and how they conspired to take over the Catholic Church. I certainly don't approve of Catholic priests abusing little boys but we were talking about homosexuality, not pedophiles, not perverts. He has conflated the two. I puzzle. Was he abused as a child by a priest, perhaps a teacher in his Catholic military school? He talks about the way homosexuals want to unravel decent society, destroy children, etc. And now I hear him. He means it. Here is the heart of the matter. And I cannot ignore his voice. I think of him in his condominium in Albany raging at the forces in society that have pulled us into a more liberal and tolerant world.

I think of him as a lion with a splinter in his paw. I would remove it if I could. But I know I can't. In order to try I would have to get very close to his fangs, his open mouth, his huge weight. I know I can't and shouldn't try. I send him an e-mail. "We have to stop writing each other. I am sorry. This will not work. This is the end." He doesn't answer. He sends me more articles from the *Weekly Standard*. The next week brings me at least fifteen more links to right-wing radio hosts and others. I understand that all over America there are people reading and believing this material. It all has a conspiratorial ring, it all rages against some liberal souls who have undermined the decent and the good. I don't read all the way through. I e-mail Albany, "Take me off this list, please." He e-mails me back, "I did," and that is that. I miss him. I miss his e-mails.

Most of all I miss the possibility of him, the visit that we never had, my walk with his dog that never took place, the weight of his body against mine, which never happened. I wonder if I cut our dance short out of fear of change. I wonder if I was right in ending it. Was I a coward? A friend tells me that he was an unsuitable man, unsuitable for me and probably anyone else. I still miss imagining him.

I have known others with his perspective. They have been my dinner partners, my friends' husbands. I have enjoyed the fresh parry and thrust of argument. I wonder if it is a sign of age that I now don't want to fight, don't like the person who arrives, ready to battle, armed with his harsh views. I have heard it all before, and now, as I hear the volcano within bubbling at its core, the molten rocks shifting in the center, the anger that runs up and down the spine, makes the tongue sharp like a razor, I no longer understand the words. Whatever I may be looking for in a man it isn't Darth Vader, and I fear Albany has gone over to the dark side.

• • •

I do not delete from my computer the photos he had sent me. Not yet.

The days seem to be getting longer again. The darkness arriving later, after the evening news. It is in the early evening, as I watch the people coming home from work, walking down the long block toward my building, as lights are turned on in the windows, as the lamp lights glow, I reach for the telephone. I need to talk about anything with anyone who will talk with me. I see the pale white moon, larger today than yesterday, hanging low above the avenue, barely above the traffic lights that change from red to green and green to red like the station lights of my brother's train set. I hear a siren wail. I used to ignore sirens, so many, so fast, appearing and disappearing in an instant. Now, I pause at each and consider, Who has had a heart attack? Who will grieve the person lying now on the ground, in a store, in a restaurant? Or has someone been hit by a car or has someone been stabbed or shot? I take a moment or two to consider all the possibilities. I listen now to the sirens, I wonder who was listening when the ambulance came roaring down our block for H.

I am thinking that perhaps all this e-mailing and meeting of strangers is a pretense, a play at living, a diversion. Perhaps I do not want to find another mate. It seems so hard to exchange stories, to reach out your hand, to listen again and again, to attempt to come closer. I know that I might step away if anyone tries to come close to me. It seems too hard to begin again, to find out what movies someone likes, what their children's names are, what memories haunt them, what enrages them, what soothes them. It seems too hard to bring someone else into my head. It is too hard to begin, to hope, to flare up one's inner fires, to daydream the furnishings of a future that within days or weeks turns to ash. I'm done. Am I really done? We'll see.

I have two new friends. They are friends of friends who live in my building. They invited me to dinner. I talked too much, I think. I was pleased to be in their home. The man is an artist and he gave me a photo-drawing he has done. It is of a jar with green paint on it. It sits disembodied on a black background. I stare and stare at it. I cannot explain why it holds me this way. Some matters are not translated into words. I am going to the framer to have it framed. It is the first thing I have owned that has not been gathered with H. at my side. He framed our drawings. He chose our drawings. I was happy at his happiness but I hardly looked. This one is mine. I am suddenly appreciative of the eyes I have to see, the hands I have to hold this piece, the space it will take on my wall.

.   .   .

I don't open any e-mails from strangers. I suspect I will not find the elusive male companion in cyberspace. It is the disappointment in Albany that has convinced me.

I have always wondered about hermits in their caves. How do their days go by? I am not a hermit. I say hello to the doorman every morning. I have a conversation with my cleaner at the corner when I drop off my cat-haired sweater. I have a long talk with a friend about a political column in the *New York Times*. I have a computer with e-mails on it from friends. I am expecting a friend from Israel to stay a few nights next week. I am having some friends over for dinner on Sunday and one of them is going to read Book Two of the new translation of *Aeneid* aloud in my living room. However, I think of myself, on my fourteenth floor, as growing moldy, undernourished, un-groomed. People make jokes about hermits. They are, to the degree that they actually exist, probably the mentally ill, the homeless, the ones hearing voices, that are on our streets, sleeping on the church steps, covered by filthy blan-kets and tattered shirts. I am not one of them. Any com-parison is melodramatic, I know. Melodrama is a bad habit of mind. It's the first baby step toward madness. I don't mind ending up dead, but I do mind ending up mad.

A friend tells me to buy some new expensive clothes. My friend says I could use sprucing up. I don't want a man who wants me only if I am spruced up. "It's just to lure him," she says. "It's just so he would want to get to know you." But I don't want a man who needs to be lured by the cut of my clothes. The issue goes deep into the vein of who I am, a natural woman, a woman without guile, at least the kind you wear. I am resistant to the idea of luring anyone. A lure contains a hook disguised by pretty feathers. The result is serious harm to the prey. Am I being stubborn about this? Am I making a mountain out of a new dress?

• • •

I've noticed that my friends are now disappearing for a few weeks at a time or more. It's not that they are abandoning me, it's that they seem to be enduring private travails. Per-haps they don't want to burden me with their own stories. They don't want to talk about MRIs for suspected malig-nancy or the agonies of a child in trouble in another state or a very old parent in need of hospice care, or a major dental problem, or a loss of a job or hip surgery. But off they go, keeping their secrets. It seems as if the element of pride, the need to appear successful in all circumstances, affects the ties that link me to my world. I know something is happening. It is hinted at, but it's not explained. I suppose this is normal. We flashed our feathers when the feathers were fit to be flashed and now in drearier days many stay indoors. Friendship needs both confidences and confidence in the other's outstretched hand. I need that far more than I need to be admired. I am no longer interested in reputations, the reviews bad or good that have accumulated over the years, the social scene.

I am the tiniest of stars in the most distant of galaxies, burned out. In part this is age, and not the kind of age where one becomes a tribal elder, bringing wisdom to the campfire. The other kind of age, where even the expensive benefit invitations with embossed fancy script, which I used to throw in the wastebasket, rarely arrive. I never properly appreciated the invitations to places I didn't want to go.

. . .

I have certainly not entered my second childhood in the Shakespearean sense. But I do notice that echoes of old events rattle in my brain. I wonder if I am especially vulnerable to unhappiness when I am alone because so many hours of my childhood were spent waiting for an adult to come near. Is there some interior accounting where the loneliness becomes more unbearable because it has been borne too much, a straw-that-breaks-the-back theory? Or is this absurd? If my iceberg father had appreciated me more would I miss H. less? I doubt it. Maybe if my father had admired me more I might have a better appreciation of myself now that H. is not here to hold me up when my knees buckle. However, given my particular childhood, I might have become a gym teacher or a blackjack dealer in Vegas or a suburban golfer with an unrequited crush on the pro.

I couldn't resist. I opened my e-mails. Someone has contacted me online. A widower. He wants fun, he says. His screen name is PlayingisGood. I read his profile. He lives in the suburbs. He is interested in all sports. He worked in business. He spends a lot of time at his gym. He is not my other half that Plato said was torn away at the beginning of time. I don't answer.

LAST NIGHT I WAS AWAKE IN THE EARLY HOURS OF THE morning. The lights on the Empire State were blurred in a haze but the red light blinking at the top of the radio tower was bright enough. The windows all around me were dark but there were lights in the large construction site a few blocks over. I could see the blue light of a large television a block away. Some insomniac was staring at a pixel screen. In Elizabethan literature sex is called "the little death," but I wonder if it isn't sleep that mimics death more accurately. It prepares us for our absence. It lets us practice being not. That is an excellent reason to avoid sleep.

Let me name my dead. H. first and foremost. H. the

one that matters above all the others. But before H. there was my mother who died so long ago. Her closet filled with cocktail party dresses, at least three ball gowns, a host of black suits and a shelf with hats and another with shoes with heels as high as they could be. She had lost the use of her arms by the time the brain tumor caused the final convulsions, so for the last month of her life the packs of Camel cigarettes she needed had been removed from the bedside. I saw her head turn looking for them, again and again. She died with her makeup on her sink, her brushes and rouges and creams for moisturizing skin on the mirrored surface of her dressing table. She died with mascara tubes half used, gels for errant curls, boxes of pins for the hair, and a repair kit for broken nails in the event that she was unable to get to the manicurist. A ruby ring rested beside the monogrammed handkerchiefs on the shelf under the table's long organdy skirt. She died as her husband's mistress waited for the telephone call announcing her death. She died with her sisters ready to take the valuables from her jewelry drawer. She died with her daughter's life in chaos. She died too young. She never knew H. She would have showered him with stock certificates and ties from Saks Fifth Avenue. She would have been content with him. She would have complained that he had no capital. She would have worried about his disinterest in wealth. But she would have liked him. I know it.

Next my father died, having remarried. His mistress got him for her own in the end. On his deathbed he told his illegitimate son that he was his real father and left him all his money, which had been my mother's money but never mind. My father died unreconciled to his own death. He died without ever having played with his granddaughters. He died without wishing to bless or be blessed. "What was wrong with him?" I asked H. H. would not use the words of his profession on the people in his life. "Not a good man," was all he said. I pushed him. "What would you label him, if he were your patient?" "He wasn't," said H. "Was he narcissistic, paranoid, borderline, all of the above?" I asked. H. said I could call him any name I liked.

I did not mourn him, although I was surprised that he had died, as if I had not believed that he was human, subject to the same ends as the rest of us.

Then a few years later my brother died of AIDS. I didn't understand him, his passions or his moods, or his fierce dislikes or his insistence on the correct pronunciation of foreign words or his hatred of H.'s profession or his contempt for athletes as well as those who liked the outdoors or animals or trees. I knew he didn't like me, not my mathematical ignorance, not my inability to speak Italian or Arabic, not my lack of attention to classical music. I knew he thought I was without merit and talked too much. I knew he didn't like my children. He pointed out their flaws frequently. But his illness was stunning in its details. It was beyond acceptance, beyond grace. He had sores in his throat and lesions on his skin and fungus grew in his left eye. He was right to rail at fate.

There was between us the childhood we shared, the names we both caught in the obituaries, Sonnenberg, Bernstein, Cowan, canasta-playing friends of our mother's, golf partners of our father. In faded photographs we each could identify the party guests at long-forgotten barbeques and birthday parties. We both had intimate knowledge of the unending hostility that raged through our home. All those things bound us together, even as they forced us apart.

H. stood beside me at my brother's grave site. I could see his anger in the way he clenched his teeth, in the whiteness of his skin, in the purple vein that throbbed on his forehead. He held my hand in his glove too tightly. My fingers were crushed. He was angry at the illness, furious at the suffering it caused, and helpless before its power. H. did not like being helpless. He was silent for hours after the burial. I am left now as the last adult alive who was witness to these events. If I doubt my memory there is no one to confirm or deny it. Someone in a family must be the last alive. The question is whether this is the first or last prize.

My father, mother, brother are not ghosts in my apartment. They do not stand at the foot of my bed and glower through the night. H. is not hovering over me either. He would if he could of course, but he can't.

When Aeneas fled Troy as it stood in flames, he carried his old father on his back and held his son by the hand. For his travels he had packed the household gods, his protections from a malevolent universe, despite the fact that his sacked city was itself evidence that these household gods might better be replaced.

Metaphorically speaking, we are all carrying our household gods, our parents on our backs and the flames behind us are not the last flames that we will see. H. tried to shield me. He did the best he could.

. . .

I am concerned about self-indulgence. It is so easy to fall into that swamp. I know ways to resist that error. If I use

fewer words I risk it less. If I bind myself to the rock of reason I will survive the inner storm. If I don't allow general-
izations, clichés, through the gates I can protect myself from
bad manners, from most sloppy thinking. But if I slam the
door too tightly on the emotions that roll in and out with
daily tides I will become robotic, mechanical, unrecogniz-
able to my own eyes and useless to anyone else. Mawkishness, murky, exaggerated emotion, insincere because it has
been heated up beyond truth, mawkishness is a sin against
the mind. H. would hate it. He preferred the Dutch masters
to the baroque Italian. He preferred Mozart above all. He
cried sometimes, at movies, at a child's illness, pretending
he was not, tears misting up his glasses. I always knew why
he was crying. Which was a good thing because he would
never have told me. I promise myself that I will censor the
sentimental in me. But I cannot depend on the fact that I
will recognize it when it comes. Self-pity is the graffiti of
the heart but not so easy to avoid. I don't want to wallow.
But I begin to see that wallowing is a chronic malady easy
to condemn and hard to cure.

.   .   .

I will never leave this apartment for another. I will leave
this apartment. Both convictions are strong and absolute
and exist side by side in my head. I cannot leave this apartment because it is the place I lived with H. His drawings
are on the wall. His robe is still in the bathroom. He was
in my bed. These are his children whose photos are everywhere. His books are on the shelves. His spices are in
the kitchen cabinet. The Persian and the Kurdish rugs we
picked out together the year we moved in are on the floor.

To leave this apartment would be to leave him, although he has left without me. To find a new apartment, a smaller one perhaps, would save me some funds and bring me into my own place, unshared, accompanied only by the memories that can be carried in my brain, not those that exist on the table or in the walls. I read the real estate section each Sunday. Perhaps I should move to a condo in South Beach or a shack in the mountains of North Carolina. Perhaps I should move to the other side of town. This city has two rivers, one on each of its sides. I now live on the west, but if I moved to the east I would be closer to the sunrise, the river would run to the sea underneath the black curved steel of the bridges. I would walk by the river and watch the barges float by. I circle advertisements with a red pen. But I do nothing else. I have not come to a decision. I am not ready to go anywhere. I could not bear to lose my home, not now, not for another one, one that would not have the scent of my life, no accumulation of secrets told, no sorrows, just walls and floors and windows. But on the other hand—

A man e-mails me from the match service. He has never been married. He lives in Roslyn, Long Island. He is a school psychologist. He sounds like a good person. He wants to travel. He likes walking in the park, so do I, but then so do most people, even serial killers enjoy a stroll in the spring. But he is looking for a woman whose outer age is a few years younger than mine. Perhaps he is older than he claims. I am not younger than I claim. I answer his e-mail. But why has he never been married? Why has he never had children? Do I really want to know the answer to this question? I fear it lies in the direction of depression or wounded expectations or anxiety uncontainable or medication needed or bad memories of childhood or war trauma and on and on my thoughts run.

How long, I wonder, does it take to know a man's unspoken thoughts? I never knew everything that passed through H.'s mind. Maybe only the tip of the proverbial iceberg. Maybe only the tip of the tip. But I did know that. He would not tell me if his cold bothered him. He would not tell me if he was worried about a child. He would not tell me if he was concerned about the tuitions or the taxes. Those were matters I guessed.

He had never learned to dance. When we tried, he stepped on my toes, bumped into me, wore a silly expression on his face that said, What on earth am I doing? He would have wanted to dance with me but his body wasn't meant for it. His mind was too present. His muscles and tendons curled too tight. But when it came to leaning against me in the movies, taking my hand when the plot thickened, bending over me when I was at work at my computer and stroking my neck, when it came to making soup for me or watering a plant on my desk, his body and mind worked together.

How long, I wonder, does it take to know when a particular man wants to go home from a party, wants to have dinner, does, does not want to talk, wants to sleep? Longer than the rest of my life, I think.

.   .   .

It snowed last night. A light snow. I heard the scraping sound of the snow trucks on the avenue. I saw the frost on the windowpanes. I felt the icy air as it slipped in beneath the crack in the window I can't seem to close all the way. On the street corners snow has piled up. I have to climb over mounds in my waterproof boots in order to make my way. The harsh, unforgiving wind blows off the river and pounds on my back.

I have breakfast with my psychoanalyst stepdaughter. We meet in a café near her apartment building. All is well with her. All is well with her children. Her life is good, perhaps it is perfect. She is going on a safari with her family in August. I tell her I am having trouble working. Writing is something I have done all my life, one paragraph after another. Now I can hardly sit before my computer for five minutes. My mind wanders away from the sentence I intended to write to a blankness, a stillness. I grow tired instantly even at nine in the morning. I am writing these pages, but slowly, like a snail. I forget from day to day what I wrote before. I repeat myself. I stare at the wall. My stepdaughter thinks I'm depressed and should now consider antidepressants. Rethink my Paxil decision. But here's the problem. I'm sure they would help. I believe in medicine. I am not for brewing teas from the bark stripped off a yew at midnight. I object to pharmacology only in its rudest advertising moments. The products are fine, the prices a different quarrel. But I can't medicate a life crisis. I can't heal a cut by sealing off my sensation of bleeding. I am tough as the clichéd nails. And if that's a lie I prefer not to know it. I want to face squarely my own life story. Is this false pride? Is this ridiculous? I would say to a friend of mine who said these words to me, "Don't be so moralistic. What is wrong with a little artificial well-being? There is no advantage to unnecessary suffering." I think that's true.

My stepdaughter thinks that. She doesn't have to tell me. I see it in her skeptical eyes. But she won't tangle with my decision either. As we are talking I feel as if I might cry. I feel tears at the corners of my eyes. I have no idea why. I do not want to cry. I am not depressed. I am sad, a condition that seems entirely reasonable under the circumstances. I can't find the napkin I need to wipe my eyes. My stepdaughter retrieves it for me from under the table.

I could go to a psychiatrist for help. But help with what? Many years ago a psychoanalyst opened up my soul and I made my way hour after hour to a more honest life. Now the doctor would simply be a comfort, an expensive comfort. It is not my unconscious that is making my days hard. It is not my past that is blocking my way. Perhaps it would help to weep a little in a safe place. I keep the possibility in reserve. Not yet. Not now.

After breakfast I walk back to my apartment. There the white rays of the sun appear between the gray clouds, a stream of light as in religious paintings, directing our eyes to the sacred in the midst of a riotous canvass. The cold air enters my lungs, and I see a puff of steam from my own breath. In the middle of the last century my mother used to be able to make smoke rings rise over my head as she exhaled, her cigarette dangling from her hand. I would count the rings, three, four, five. She could shuffle the cards and make them flip through the air and return neatly into a pack. She was afraid of flying, elevators that were not operated manually by a man in uniform, tunnels, germs on toilet seats, all bridges, dogs, cats, thunder and lightning, especially lightning. I, on the other hand, fear nothing, not even death.

Not true, I fear living too long, expiring in a nursing home after a stroke that takes away my speech. I fear that time is running out. But the truth is I fear all that in a vague way, similar to my belief in the 1950s that the Russians would one day drop an A-bomb on American shores.

I see a double stroller with sleeping twin babies, bundled up to their chins. How lovely they are, a common enough sight on the Upper West Side of Manhattan. I see a little Chinese girl and her blond mother late for school.

As I walk, passing the Lebanese stationery, the discount clothing store, the flower stand, I feel restored, my arms are moving briskly. I am warm enough in my coat, my legs are going fast, over the already soot-stained snow blocking the crossings, I can feel the cold on my ears. They must have turned red, the sting is not unpleasant. I am riding time, I am watching the babies on their morning journey to the bagel store. I am watching the man with all his shirts over his arm enter the cleaners. I am still a part of it. I go shopping at a store on Broadway and find three wool sweaters and a skirt with brown polka dots, for the spring. It will be spring. These are the first clothes I have bought that H. will not have seen me wear. Inevitable that sooner or later my wardrobe would change. I will go home and call another of my daughters and talk about the school choices for my youngest grandchild and I will write about my morning, all of it.

•   •   •

I go to a Sunday luncheon party. Only couples and two gay men. We argue about the worth of this or that presidential candidate. We talk of housing bubbles and theater and the

Oscars. We talk about war, but what is there to say about war, about this war that so shames us? Someone speaks of the end of our democracy.

Someone speaks of torture and the shredded Bill of Rights. The people of Iraq are dying by the score. H. would have looked longingly at the television screen behind whose gray face some ball game was awaiting his attention. He truly believed in the discontents of civilization, the ever-erupting savage mind. He truly wanted to watch the Sunday football game. I miss his mind, ego, id and superego, all of it.

· · ·

I envy those who believe in a world to come. I envy those who believe that justice will come in the afterlife. I know that most of the world believes in some version of this story. It is hard to face death as an unending absence. But H. is altogether gone. He is not in heaven. He is not in hell. He is not waiting for his bones to come together and rise again from the valleys of Jerusalem. I think this now without pain. I think this the way one notices that it is raining outside and an umbrella will be necessary. I have developed a thick skin, or at least a usable scab. Or am I bluffing?

· · ·

Out my window on the fire escape of the building next door I see a red cardinal, a male, a small streak of rusty red moving from rung to rung. He must live in the nearby park. He may be lost or he may not be. Where is his mate? Has he lost his mate? It must be a sign of approaching spring that he comes so close. I have never seen a cardinal here

before. There is rain hitting on the windowpane. I look
down toward Broadway and see the sheepdog that lives in
the neighborhood. His owner stops to talk to a passerby.
The dog wags his tail. I can see even from the fourteenth
floor the dog is pleased. The rain falls on them all.

. . . .

A letter comes in the mail from old friends from Boston,
whom thirty years ago we met on vacation in Nantucket
when all our children were young. I have only seen them
once or twice since then. It isn't Christmas or New Year's,
which is the usual time for such communications. The letter encloses a family picture. Lovely mother and father,
two grown children each with their mates and three little
children, grandchildren. The letter explains that the parents are still at work, the father as a neurosurgeon at a major hospital, the mother in a mental health organization.
The daughter works for a private foster care group and the
son-in-law is a journalist and the son is a paramedic and
his Italian wife is expecting another baby. The faces beam
out of the photograph. The background shows a living
room with French doors opening onto a garden. A large
fern plant has not a brown edge on a single leaf. Congratulations are in order. Congratulations for having raised a
good family, because the children all live within a mile
of each other and their parents, because there has been
no divorce, no major illness, no misfortune that is visible on the faces in the photo. Because decent people have
managed to survive the years looking pleased, because no
child was afflicted with autism, no cancer cells took a life,
no one fell into the pit of addiction or smoked till lungs

burned. I stare at the picture. Why now? What is wrong that the mother and the father needed to send this picture now? What lurks under the couch? What haunts the bright smile of the mother? Is this a competitive missive? *Look how much better my family is than yours, you, opener of my letter, read it and feel bad because your happiness can't measure up to ours.* More likely this letter was created in the boiler room of insecurity. *Look, I have a good family too, just as good as I imagine yours to be.*

This may not be the right way to read this letter. Most likely it was sent in some spirit of good will, a reaching out to old friends who do not live in the neighborhood. If H. were here he would either agree with my suspicions or not. He would ask me what mean-spirited thoughts are running through my head that I would consider this letter as if it were a gauntlet thrown on my table. He would think the sin of competitiveness mine, cast out against my correspondent. And so I suppose it is. He is not here so I have to figure out on my own that my family photo would have an empty space where he should be standing. It would show a divorced child. If our photo had a Dorian Gray magic it would be fading out, black and white, and we would all have deep shadows under our eyes. This hurts.

But that is beside the point. No photo could show the way our children, all but one, have stood with me, have moved in their own lives outward, how we have managed. I send the mother of the family in Boston a letter. "Bravo," I say. But as I put it in the mail I wonder, what is wrong in that house?

●   ●   ●

My nephew calls. I have not spoken to him for over ten years. We agree to meet for coffee. There he is at the table. Love and guilt rise in me. Tentatively, anxiously, with great unease, we talk. A need not to feel guilt rushes over me. I want to tell him something important but I can't find the words. "Forgive me" would do. I hope he hears those words behind the lines of words I actually say. We talk of his work, his life. He walks me home to my apartment building. Now he is back in my life. Now I am back in his. Is this the way two birds might cross in the same sky, wings not touching, in an instant each out of sight of the other? Or not?

• • •

It is Saturday and I have nothing to do until Sunday at one o'clock. At one o'clock on Sunday I'm having lunch with a man who contacted me on Match.com. At four o'clock on Sunday I am seeing my stepdaughter and her family and at seven o'clock I am having dinner with friends. But today is empty. I could have prevented this by calling this one or that one and making an arrangement, a movie to be seen, a lunch somewhere, but I thought enough is enough. I should manage a day or more by myself. After all, the other night after dinner some forty blocks away I got on the subway and came home without a fear, without a tremble, easily as if I had always gone everywhere at night alone.

I could read, I will try to read. I could go for a long walk. I will go for a long walk. Years ago when the children were very young we went each Saturday to the zoo. We bought kibble for them to feed the goats. We went to the carousel and H. would sit on a horse and go round and round with one daughter or another on his lap. The younger one wanted to ride by herself. The older one had to be coaxed and sat on her father's lap with her lips pursed together and her body braced for disaster. I thought that I would spend every Saturday of my life at the zoo. But that phase passed and other phases passed, and now I am looking at the hours of the day as if they were endless dunes in an endless desert. There is nothing to do but start forward.

I am meeting the psychologist from Long Island. He has never been married or had children but seems to want a relationship, late of course for this desire. I wonder what kept him single so long. He will have a story, a long story. I am curious but wary. Why is he looking for a companion now in his late life? Is he wanting someone to take care of him? It is unkind of me to think of this. If I begin to view approaching men as if they are predators then I will be ever alone, and not because it was fate or accident or anything of the sort. It will be because my soul soured before its time, my capacity to greet the world curdled. I called him at the number he sent me. Who knows, we may enjoy each other.

Sunday—I meet C. at a local café. He has traveled on the train to meet me. I can't help the trace of hope that rises as I close my door behind me. I try to ignore it, but it follows me up the block. He is standing outside the café when I arrive, waiting for me. He is a gentle, sad man with dark, bushy eyebrows, an ex-boxer's face, a wide chest; a child's mischievousness plays across his mouth. We talk easily with each other. He wants to know me. He has read a book of mine. He asks the right questions, the ones that tell him where I came from, what has happened to me.

I ask him the same questions. He is not eager to tell me anything beyond the bare details but I persist. Who were his parents, I ask. He moves his coffee from one side of the table to the other. He shrugs.

Does it matter in our adult life if a person is born and raised in a very different place from you? I don't think so. Finally C. tells me that he was raised in six different foster homes and separated from his identical twin at age seven. He spent five years in an institution for troubled boys. His childhood is one that Oliver Twist would recognize. His adult years had been a struggle, to finish college which he didn't do until his thirties, to find a profession, to make a place for himself, and in the course of all that he never found a woman, a woman he could trust or share his life with. And now? Now it may be too late. He loves to walk on the beach, to read, to listen to music, but I wonder if the wounds are not still festering?

Also it may be too late for me to ever hold another man's hand and think nothing of it, to walk beside him and know how his steps will fall. Is there a time when you can transplant your roots and another time when habits and custom and attachment to the old bind you, block you, keep you alone? I am not sure if I want to hold C.'s sad story in my crowded mind. I consider that I may die alone, pressing the life-alert button on the buzzer I will wear around my neck because I am afraid of strays with bleary eyes and men with long, sad histories. I am not sure about C. When I think of explaining myself to him, explaining my children, I sigh. He asks me if I would like to take a trip to Vietnam with him. I would and I wouldn't. I won't.

•   •   •

I am a hippopotamus sleeping in the mud. I must rouse myself, but the mud is what I know, the mud is warm and will not kill me. I can look at the familiar bush to the left and I can smell the familiar dead fish to the right and I can let the bird sit on my head if it should wish to pause in its flight. The effort to rise up and charge forward on my fat, stumpy hippopotamus legs seems more than should be required of an ordinary creature. I endure the sun. I wait for the rain to wash the dust from my hanging cheeks. Perhaps my blood pressure is low. Perhaps my potassium is low. Perhaps I have lost my nerve. No one ever said that nerve is a boundless renewable source.

Once I wore a red pinny and chased down the field swinging a hockey stick, back and forth after a tiny white ball all afternoon. Now I could nap from noon to sunset. Now I see no point in running until my chest is tight with pain. I see no point. Possibly because I lack teammates.

I pick up a copy of *New York* magazine and in the back I see two pages of advertisements for matchmakers. They promise to help you find your mate, any age twenty-five to seventy-five. They promise to be discreet. They promise a private meeting. This differs from e-mail matching only in that a real person (whose face is grinning at me from the ad) has to learn my name and cash my check for the service. How many disconnected people must there be in the world if a full two pages' worth of matchmaking companies buy space to hawk their services. I can't do this. Why not? Because I am a widow not a wallflower. While there is no label for male wallflowers, I suspect that the users of these services would qualify for the description. On the other hand this is a distinction without a purpose.

Perhaps I am living in an age that has passed. There may no longer be parents and siblings and friends to introduce the single to each other. Our circles while larger may be weaker. It may take a village to introduce a widow to a widower but I don't live in a village. Should I move to one?

·   ·   ·

I have guests coming. I open the cookbook and a recipe written on a scrap of paper falls out. It is H.'s handwriting, his illegible doctor's scrawl. It is a recipe for glazed carrots. A wall tumbles down. I cannot stop the tears. Over a recipe? I attempt to distract myself. I pick up the newspaper. A levee has been breached: more tears. All right. I give in. This will be a morning of tears, tears without reason, tears that rise and flood, recede and rise again. I suspect tears. But what can I do, they have arrived. I trust they will go. I could call a friend. I don't. These tears are not matters for a friend. They are private. Just between H. and me. Which under the circumstances means just for me. Tears do not wash away the debris they bring any more than rain empties the sky of water. I go to my desk. "Welcome," says my computer. Writing stops the tears: immediately. I would never risk harm to my computer. Water might seep in and destroy a chip, an electronic pulse, a necessary connection. I type dry-eyed. I have restored the levee.

A man has e-mailed me. I read his profile. He sounds sweet. He lives in another state. He is a golf player. He talks of love. I'll think about him later.

·   ·   ·

Some dear friends know a single divorced man around my age. Some years ago he left a wife, a fine-looking, intelligent woman, the mother of his daughter, and married a very young, long-legged Frenchwoman with whom he has a child now seven years old. The mother of the child has grown tired of him and wants to live alone with her child in Paris. I envy this man his seven-year-old son. I envy this man his ability to play in the fields of beauty and youth as long as it pleases him. The man knows me but doesn't call. I am sorry that this man cannot see me. Once I was a long-legged girl, but "once" is not much of an invitation into the present.

I go with a cousin to see an apartment she might purchase in a neighborhood building. The apartment is on a high floor with views of the cathedral and the church steeple and the looping bridge across the river. We visit a friend of hers who lives in the building. The woman is about my age, a widow too, but she tells us that she is meeting her boyfriend in a few minutes. He has been introduced to her by her children who went to school with his children. She has his picture by her bed on the opposite side of her dead husband's photo. I am jealous. She beams, she glows, she is joyous. Is this luck? I have never really believed in luck. A good man does not just fall out of the sky. You need to make such a thing happen. You need to be ready if such a thing does happen. You can't be mean and grouchy, bitter or sad. You need to be able to catch your luck. When I was a child the carousel in Central Park had a wooden arm on its side from which rings hung and you could lean off your horse and reach for a ring. If you caught a gold one you could ride twice more for free. I would swing from my horse, one hand around its painted neck, time it as best I could, and extend my arm as far as it would go, the wooden beams of the building went up and down with the motion of the horses. But you had to reach and sometimes you missed and for years my arms were too short and when they were long enough the game was no longer so interesting.

At any rate I am jealous. A strange feeling I can hardly remember from girlhood. A knot forms in my chest. I smile at the woman. The loss of innocence occurs more than once.

· · ·

The red cardinal has returned, his brown mate with him. They fly high above the garbage cans in the alley below. They stop to rest on windowsills and on the bars of the fire escape. He pecks her on the neck. She flies a few feet away. I throw open the window. The air is warmer than it has been. The season is changing. I am going around but not forward. Or perhaps I am. The roots under the dark ground bulge and push, long before a green shoot breaks the surface.

There was an architect who designed a beautiful synagogue near the sea in the town where once we vacationed. The synagogue was made of glass and a glowing honey-colored wood, pure as we all wish our hearts could be. Something however was wrong with the architect. One afternoon he went for a swim in the ocean on a deserted beach and he took off his clothes and folded them neatly next to his towel and went into the water and swam out to sea and when he could swim no longer he sank. It could be that he thought he would never build anything to equal his synagogue. Or more likely a depression with a monster's face overcame him one morning at the breakfast table as he was pouring milk on his cereal. Perhaps his wife planned to leave him or he had just received a diagnosis of liver cancer or early Alzheimer's. The local papers had no answer, or if they had it, they didn't print it.

I think of myself in the ocean, the tide pulling me outwards, my limbs numb with the cold, the ocean is always cold. I brush away the seaweed that clings to my leg as if I were a log floating by. I open my eyes under the water but I see no fish, only the tiny debris of cell life, fish gill, spittle of ocean creatures. Do I want to get back to shore now that I have gone so far out that I cannot turn around? No one sees me. No one waves. At the horizon's edge I see a boat, a fishing boat with trawler nets raised high. It is too far away for me to hail. I do not want to hail it. I drift. My arms are tired, my muscles ache. Virginia Woolf put stones in her pockets so she would quickly drop to the bottom. In an ocean it would be important to start at high tide, to swim out, far over one's head, where you can't put feet down and reverse direction at will. Is Spain really over there out beyond the edge, which isn't an edge but just a curve, an illusion of a stopping place, a separation of sky and land?

·   ·   ·

I have an idea for a story. I keep the idea in a special place in my brain and I pull it out every once in a while to examine it, expand it, let it breathe. I am having friends over for dinner. I buy a piece of salmon from the fish store. I walk along Broadway and see that under the awnings of the Korean stores the daffodils are now sitting in buckets of water. There they are, a humble flower, cheap, persistent, yellow, a flower of the proletariat. I purchase a bunch along with green leaves. At home I place them in a glass vase in the middle of my dining table. My cat tries to eat the leaves. I chase him away. I know that as soon as my back is turned he will return to his feast and my flowers will not last the night. A cat is entitled to some pleasure too, a splash of color in his life, a leaf or two to munch. I understand. I speak to my daughters on the phone. They report no disasters, no new wounds of mind or body. This is good.

                            .   .   .

I wake at 2:45 in the morning. It is dark, but not dead dark, dark on the edge of mitigation. I no longer put my hand out to feel the empty space next to me. I know it is there. I listen to the sirens wail along the avenue. I pick up my *New Yorker* magazine. I want to read an article about the Sudan. But I am too tired. My head begins to throb. I cannot help those the Janjaweed would kill. I cannot make dictators desist and warlords retreat and land-grabbers grow modest in their needs. I am a widow who can grind her teeth in fury, who can write a letter to her president, e-mail a friend, or just wait for morning at the window, knowing that the blush of dawn will return over the East River when it is ready, good and ready and nothing I can do will rush the morning, or change the drip-drip of time, or rescue a child. Then I read an article about aging. I read about a woman in her eighties who lives alone and due to arthritis and stiffness in the joints has not been able to clean her own feet, so they have grown filthy, infected, cracked. She also forgets to eat and drink. Otherwise she's fine. What upsets me more than her feet are the empty days she describes with no one coming to visit, no work to do, no one expecting her call. I don't want my arteries kept open longer than my telephone lines.

So I consider the matter of my own body. It is still hale. I can bend and swoop and my knees are willing and my arms while not rippling with muscle are up to most tasks. My heart beats steadily. My eyes are clear. My ears hear. My fingers have no swelling in the joints, my legs are still firm. But I know the odds. A small vessel in my brain will break off from its branch and spill blood where blood does not belong. Or a clot in an artery will break loose and, like a hand over a mouth, the words will end. I will grow nauseous and break out in sweat and exhaustion will roll over me and I will or will not be near enough a hospital. Perhaps a cell will lose its fight with an antagonist and turn into its own enemy and replicate its cannibalistic self somewhere, breast, liver, pancreas, intestine, gland, frontal lobe. No matter how vigilant I am, how regularly I take my aspirin, take my vitamins, abstain from evil substances, the thing will happen. In the early hours of the morning when the street is mostly still, the lamp lights fuzzy in the dimness, the stars paled, the moon out of my sight, I can tell something is approaching. I'm waiting for it to announce itself. Whom will I call when it comes? Who will comfort me? I practice comforting myself, with reassuring words, with a drink of water, with a hand on the cat's head. I might welcome the intruder when it comes. I could be ready. I could be waiting with my ticket in hand on the railroad platform for the last trip. I could hear the train whistle blowing down the track and with only a small shiver of fear, a wave of my hand to my daughters, move eagerly forward as the bells of the lowering guard gate sound.

Also I haven't forgotten my window, the one that opens to the alley below. If I am not paralyzed or too weak to turn the handle on the window's frame, I can avoid the worst. If I have the courage. If I don't then I deserve what will follow.

.   .   .

In the afternoon I go to a concert with friends. I hear music now better than I ever did before H.'s death. I don't know why but I guess that it is because music reaches behind or over words and words are less insistent in my brain, I can't tell H. anything. This leaves a space for music to climb into my brain. At any rate I am grateful. Then last night I saw a wonderful movie. I wished I had written the script for that movie. I wished I had directed that movie. I could never have written that movie. It was about Spain at the end of the Civil War and about a child and the Resistance and an evil Fascist. (That is and is not an oxymoron.) It was a fairy tale. But you needed to know different things than I know in order to have written that story. Or is that an excuse? When I was younger I would have said, I can do that in my own vocabulary. Now I think I have such a limited vocabulary. Or has my imagination become ossified? Will it revive? I wished H. had seen that movie with me.

In the shower my mind drifts back to that lawsuit, settled some months ago. I was attacked. I felt attacked. If I were a cartoon figure, a bite would be taken out of my head. Not a large bite, significant only because I would look lopsided. The bite is not financial although that too.

It is about having left, in my slimy snail-like trail, a really bad enemy. It's about admitting the limits of my capacity to skip about gracefully. When I think of that lawsuit I feel ugly. Although I did nothing wrong, I did nothing extraordinarily right either. I imagine most people carry around a story or two like this. Not necessarily a lawsuit, but something that sticks in the craw, forms a burr on the bone, makes the soul creak as if it were older than it is. That is how we know we've fallen from grace, been expelled from the garden.

I have been contacted on Match.com by someone who calls himself Longingforyou. I can't. I just can't respond. Perhaps Longingforyou is my perfect mate, perhaps I am closing doors that I should leave open. But I can't walk through that one. Also the same morning comes an e-mail from Friskyatnight. He is thirty-two years old and is looking for a woman from fifty to seventy years of age. The secret fantasies we all hold, fantasies that once would have remained in our brains, are now taken out for a vast Internet show-and-tell. This is interesting: inhibition may become a fossil found only in Amish communities. Repression may have gone the way of the dial telephone.

I find I do not immediately throw in the trash the brochures for trips that arrive from museums and alumna associations. I read them carefully. I daydream myself in faraway places listening to lectures on sculpture or the life of the starfish. I think about Paris and Florence and the rivers in Montana. Eventually after the brochures have sat on my table for several weeks I scoop them up and toss them out. But I am getting closer to packing a suitcase and going somewhere.

IN THE JEWISH TRADITION, ON THE ANNIVERSARY OF A death there is a ceremony held at the grave site and the stone is unveiled and the family comes to see the stone at the grave site and prayers are said. H.'s death was in December but a year later the ground was frozen and it wasn't possible to mount the stone. We waited until April. It is warm and the sun is welcome after weeks of rain, after a winter of a harsh wind blowing off the river. We drive in two cars, my children and their children, and we go to the cemetery some fifty minutes away. I wear my sunglasses. I need to protect my eyes from the sight of others. I need to protect others from the sight of my eyes. In the back of the minivan in which I am sitting, the son of my stepdaughter, my oldest grandchild, who has come down from college for the occasion, is discussing his girlfriend, who lives in Los Angeles. The subject turns to the Mets game the night before. His mother leans forward from her seat in the far back wanting to hear every word. His little sister is drawing on a pad in her lap. The middle child has barely opened his eyes, that sixteen-year-old mask on his face tells me nothing. I want to tell my son-in-law to drive me back home. I want to tell them I changed my mind. The other car with my two daughters, one husband and two little girls has already arrived at our destination and waits for us at the cemetery gates. I have arranged this not because of custom or religious law, neither of which would have impressed H. and neither of which binds me. I planned this excursion to the grave site. I must have had a reason. I search my mind but can't find it. I say nothing and the car moves up the highway toward the cemetery.

We arrive. The cemetery gate is wide open. Furious barking comes from three large dogs penned in a cage. In Greek mythology the dog Cerberus guards the gates to Hades. I think of the river Styx, which brings the dead to the shores of the afterlife where they will reside, shades, shadows, nonlives, ever after. These dogs are not mythological. They must be there to frighten grave robbers or more likely grave vandals. We ignore them and take our cars up the hill toward the top where a group of graves, a few newly dug, soft brown dirt marking the spots, wait. Most have large marble markers with names and dates and a few words on them. My oldest grandson finds the grave we are looking for and we walk over to the site. A white cloth is taped across the face of the stone. My son-in-law takes off the tape and removes the tape dispenser, a green plastic tongue, which was left on the ledge. The little girls are strangely quiet, hanging on to any hand offered. I give all of the grandchildren small rocks that H. and I had brought back from the Rainbow River in Alaska, where he had caught his biggest salmon, the one he was most proud of. I remember him holding it in his arms, almost too heavy for him, water dripping from its gills, blood visible on the jawline and the glassy eyes staring, not at the camera but at eternity. I remember the silver gills, a few shedding from the fish onto his yellow rubber boots. Each child places one of the stones on the edge of the monument. The words can be read in black chiseled letters, and in the line below are the dates of his life, its beginning and its end.

We say three psalms, all of us reading them together. We say the Kaddish. We stand a moment or more. Suddenly I remember the sound that came from H.'s throat as he stumbled up the steps of our lobby and collapsed on the floor beside me. It was a moan, but not a moan. It was a reedy sound, like that of a loon from across a lake in Maine. It was like the wind entangled in the branches of an old oak tree. It was like nothing I had ever heard before, this sound. Perhaps it was simply the air rushing out of lungs, the compression of the throat from the sudden constriction of muscles. I hear this sound again standing by the grave site. I don't actually hear it. I remember it, which is close enough to cause a trembling in my legs. I will not tremble. The little girls are now running about on the grass. I am of two minds. I would like to stay and stay by his grave. I would like to leave immediately. We have paused before the omniscient eye of the universe long enough. Faintly at a great distance I hear the dogs still barking.

I am not overcome with emotion. I am numb. I look out over the landscape, under the rising power lines, which swoop up the nearby hill and down the next one. I see graves as far as the eye can see. The commonality of death calms me. The grief of it all is absent from the warm spring air. The new grass is growing even in the freshly dug earth. My three-year-old granddaughter asks her mother, "When people die do they still have selfs?" Her mother says, "I don't know." I know but I wouldn't tell a three-year-old.

On the way back to the city, leaving the cemetery behind, leaving my own grave, a plot beside H., to lie empty a while longer, I find tears leaking out from beneath the rim of my sunglasses. Why? No new sorrow has come my way. No new loss has hit me. I can tolerate tombs and marble stones and grass plots and cemeteries with open gates. I can accept the fact of death, even my own, with calm. I can accept that there is nothing or almost nothing left of H. by now. So then why the tears, which I have trouble stopping and must stop because we are going to have a picnic in the park and I don't want my family to find my face wet with tears.

Who cares if I cry, I think. I imagine there are other families in which the widow might wail at the grave site, might weep loudly for hours, her children's hands on her shoulders, hugging her, their own tears and loud cries mingling with hers. There is nothing wrong with that scene, I watch it on television as it is broadcast from Iraq daily, but it is not our way. My children would be embarrassed if they saw me crying. I would be embarrassed by my red nose and my hurt eyes. I would feel vulnerable and even here with my children I need a face, a face to hide behind. I consider this in the car as we are driving and tears are falling despite my effort to stop them, despite my effort to discover the reason or unreason for them, exactly. I am supposed to be the mother, the one that protects the children. If I am unraveling that will frighten them. But they are old enough to understand, old enough to tolerate my tears without fears that something will collapse beneath their feet. But I can't shed my disguise. I struggle to regain composure. Then my son-in-law who is driving perhaps sees out of the corner of his eye my red nose, my leaking tears. He asks me when I first met H. He knows the story. But I start to tell him anyway. And in the telling the tears stop. Why, I don't know. But I have to select my words, pace my tale, color in the details. I am a storyteller after all. I grow animated with description. I am involved in telling. I am not weeping. I tell him about the party I was supposed to go to that night forty-one years ago but didn't go to because H. had asked me out to a movie and sounded so shy on the telephone that I thought he might not call back if I refused his first invitation.

If anyone had said, "I know you must feel sad, seeing the grave," I would have wept. So I am glad no one did. If anyone had said, "You must miss him," I would have wept. No one did. They must have received signals from me that I would not want them to come so near. There was a time in their lives years ago, their teenage years, when everything I did embarrassed them, but now it was my own wish to remain dignified that kept me quiet and contained.

Dignity, what is it but a wall that blocks out, that locks in.

I think about my mother. She died forty-four years ago. I had been in a black limousine provided by the funeral home when we came down the same highway I was on now. I don't remember the name of the cemetery. It was March and there had been a winter storm a few days before. White mounds of snow clung to the sides of the highway and the trees were barren. She never knew H. or her grandchildren.

Back in the city we go to the park carrying bread and cheese and homemade cookies and sesame noodles in containers and seltzer and water and we sit on the grass under a blossoming cherry tree and we eat and drink. The little girls run around playing hide-and-seek behind the trunks of trees from which they were never hidden. The littlest one tries to hide by pulling her dress over her head. We laugh.

Alone in my apartment I walk from room to room. Wherever I sit I am uncomfortable and move somewhere else. What I would like is a summer camp for adults my age, with a communal dining room and taps at night and weekly movies and campfires and songs and a hike to a place where a stream runs down between high rocks and birch bark and pinecones fall on the dark soil that crunches underfoot. But such a place if it existed would be filled with the near-blind, the hardly hearing, the limping, the sad, the lonely, the diseased or about to be diseased. It would be hard to keep up one's courage there. And after years of living in one small place with many of the same people with the same politics, same professions, with the same favorite restaurants, how easy would it be to go elsewhere? A summer camp that never ends is not such a good idea.

I revisit the idea of selling this apartment and moving away. I once again read the real estate section of the newspaper looking for places in the northern woods, places near the ocean, places where the sun shines all year, places where I could go and start again. I read the prices. I compare them. I wonder if I could really go and if I went would I sit alone wherever I was. A friend calls. We talk about a movie we had both seen the week before. It was a good conversation. I am all right after all. I do not need a male, or a partner, to make me complete. I am good enough as is. I am through with e-mails and matches online. If love should come to me again I would welcome it. If I am without love ever after I can console myself with the thought

that ever after is not so long now and that my memory is
good and can comfort me if I need comforting.

THERE IS A GREEK MYTH ABOUT AN OLD COUPLE, BAUCIS
and Philomen, who live in a poor hut on the edge of the
forest. The god Hermes comes to visit them and they offer
him some of the milk that sits in the pitcher on their table.
They offer him bread and shelter. The Olympian sees how
poor they are and is grateful for the kindness of the simple
man and woman he sees before him. He reveals himself
as a god and tells them he will grant any wish they have.
They ask him to allow them to die at the same moment, so
that one will not have to suffer without the other. Hermes
agrees. A while later they both die in the same instant and
their bodies are instantly transformed into two trees that
grow toward the sky side by side with their branches in-
tertwined and the wind touching their leaves and the sun
rushing down to warm their bark. Unlikely story that. But
I understand the wish that prompted that tale. Widowhood, as I am now growing accustomed to it, can be a calm
place. I can pretend I am a tree with my branches locked in
another tree. I will be a tree that can bend with the wind
and survive a great storm.

I go to a concert for young artists and hear an amazing
pianist play Mozart. The lights in the theater remind me of
the candles we set in soap bars and sent out into the lake

long ago when I was a child. The stars above watched over my candle or so it seemed to my innocent eyes. Tonight the lights shimmer and fade against the crystal and the gold that line the tiers of red velvet seats. The audience barely breathes. The pianist bends and waves above the keys, his long arms reaching like the wings of a bird.

I walk along Broadway and pass flowers in buckets in front of the Asian greengrocer. Among them I see tiny orchids on a long thin branch. I look at the pale petals, pinkish at the center, white in the middle and then almost purple at the ends. What a miracle a flower is. I buy three branches just for myself. These shapes and colors are not miracles, I know. I really do know. These qualities came about through the ages to attract insects, to survive predators, to secure the sunshine, all for the purpose of spreading themselves across a field. Nevertheless the bundle in my arms, wrapped in a white cheap paper with a vine-like design across it, is proof that sorrow is only a slice of the story and the other portion is brilliant in the sunshine, gentle in the dusk and perfect in my arms.

I do not have my soul mate and most likely will never have another but I will be fine. I can read. I can think. I can work. I can see friends. I can watch my grandchildren grow. I can walk in the park and I can listen to music and I can argue politics and I can pass, if fate allows it, from old to older in the usual manner. I will be sad often but not always. I will be lonely most always but not unbearably so. I will look forward to small things, a dinner with friends, a movie, the first orange persimmons. I will miss sex. I will miss conversations after midnight with the covers pulled up tight across the chest to keep the warmth inside while cold air frosts the windowpanes. I will have no one to tell good news or bad. I will miss the unsaid things that passed between H. and me. But I will manage without them. I will make new friends in unexpected places. I will take a trip somewhere I have always wanted to go. I will not let grief become my constant companion. I will refuse its offer to accompany me to the corner, to the night, to the next month.

If the owl and the pussycat went to sea in a pea-green boat and the owl flew off, the pussycat better pick up the oars and row toward shore—she has, after all, neither wings nor gills. She must dance by herself by the light of the moon.